SCULPTURE

MATERIALS, TECHNIQUES, STYLES, AND PRACTICE

EDITED BY
CLEO KUHTZ

Britannica
Educational Publishing
IN ASSOCIATION WITH

ROSEN
EDUCATIONAL SERVICES

Published in 2017 by Britannica Educational Publishing (a trademark of Encyclopædia Britannica, Inc.) in association with The Rosen Publishing Group, Inc.
29 East 21st Street, New York, NY 10010

Distributed exclusively by Rosen Publishing.
To see additional Britannica Educational Publishing titles, go to rosenpublishing.com.

First Edition

Britannica Educational Publishing
J.E. Luebering: Executive Director, Core Editorial
Anthony L. Green: Editor, Compton's by Britannica

Rosen Publishing
Kathy Campbell: Senior Editor
Nelson Sá: Art Director
Michael Moy: Designer
Cindy Reiman: Photography Manager
Carina Finn: Photo Researcher
Supplementary material by Cleo Kuhtz

Library of Congress Cataloging-in-Publication Data

Names: Kuhtz, Cleo, editor.
Title: Sculpture : materials, techniques, styles, and practice / Edited by Cleo Kuhtz.
Description: First Edition. | New York : Britannica Educational Publishing in Association with Rosen Educational Services, 2017. | Series: Britannica's Practical Guide to the Arts | Includes bibliographical references and index.
Identifiers: LCCN 2015048113 | ISBN 9781680483758 (library bound : alk. paper)
Subjects: LCSH: Sculpture--Technique--Juvenile literature. | Artists' materials--Juvenile literature.
Classification: LCC NB1143 .S38 2016 | DDC 730.28--dc23
LC record available at http://lccn.loc.gov/2015048113

Manufactured in China

CONTENTS

INTRODUCTION viii

CHAPTER ONE
THE ELEMENTS AND PRINCIPLES OF SCULPTURAL DESIGN 1
ELEMENTS OF DESIGN 1
PRINCIPLES OF DESIGN 6
    CONTRAPPOSTO 9
    FORESHORTENING 13
RELATIONSHIPS TO OTHER ARTS 14

CHAPTER TWO
MATERIALS OF SCULPTURE AND THEIR CONSERVATION AND REPAIR 17
PRIMARY 17
    MARBLE 20
    DAVID SMITH 28
    TERRA-COTTA 32
    PLASTER OF PARIS 38
SECONDARY 39
    PAPIER-MÂCHÉ 41
CONSERVATION AND RESTORATION OF SCULPTURE 42
  STONE SCULPTURE 43
  METAL SCULPTURE 51
  WOOD SCULPTURE 54

CHAPTER THREE
METHODS AND TECHNIQUES 57
    REPOUSSÉ 58

THE SCULPTOR AS DESIGNER
AND AS CRAFTSMAN............................. 58
GENERAL METHODS 61
CARVING 63
  INDIRECT CARVING 64
  CARVING TOOLS AND TECHNIQUES 65
    A FILE................................... 67
MODELING 69
    AN ARMATURE 70
  MODELING FOR CASTING 70
  MODELING FOR POTTERY SCULPTURE 72
  GENERAL CHARACTERISTICS OF
  MODELED SCULPTURE......................... 73
CONSTRUCTING AND ASSEMBLING 73
DIRECT METAL SCULPTURE 75
REPRODUCTION AND
SURFACE-FINISHING TECHNIQUES 76
    THE LOST-WAX PROCESS 77
  CASTING AND MOLDING 78
  POINTING 81
  SURFACE FINISHING 82
    ABOUT GILDING........................... 85
    ANODIZING 88

CHAPTER FOUR

FORMS, SUBJECT MATTER, IMAGERY, AND SYMBOLISM OF SCULPTURE

FORMS, SUBJECT MATTER, IMAGERY,
AND SYMBOLISM OF SCULPTURE........ 89
SCULPTURE IN THE ROUND 89
    *THE GREAT PHIDIAS AND
    THE PARTHENON SCULPTURES*........... 92
RELIEF SCULPTURE 95
    INTAGLIO................................. 98
MODERN FORMS OF SCULPTURE................100
    ENVIRONMENTAL SCULPTURE............103

REPRESENTATIONAL SCULPTURE 105

   THE HUMAN FIGURE 106

   DEVOTIONAL IMAGES AND
   NARRATIVE SCULPTURE 107

   PORTRAITURE 109

   SCENES OF EVERYDAY LIFE 109

   ANIMALS 109

   FANTASY 110

   OTHER SUBJECTS 111

NONREPRESENTATIONAL SCULPTURE 112

DECORATIVE SCULPTURE 113

SYMBOLISM 114

      THE TYMPANUM 117

CHAPTER FIVE
USES OF SCULPTURE 120

DECORATIONS 120

ARCHITECTURE 120

GARDENS AND PARKS .121

COMMEMORATIONS 122

      JEAN-ANTOINE HOUDON 122

COINAGE AND MEDALS 124

GLYPTIC ARTS 125

CEREMONIES AND RITUALS 125

CHAPTER SIX
THE HISTORY OF SCULPTURE 126

SCULPTURE AMONG EARLY PEOPLES 126

      *THE ARCHAEOLOGICAL
      SITE AT TULA* 128

THE ART OF EGYPT 130

MESOPOTAMIA AND ITS ART 131

AFRICAN SCULPTURE 131

ASIAN SCULPTURE 134
THE GLORIOUS SCULPTURE OF GREECE 137
     PRAXITELES 139
FROM THE ROMANS TO THE RENAISSANCE 141
CHRISTIANITY AND A NEW ART 142
     TILMAN RIEMENSCHNEIDER 143
THE RENAISSANCE IN ITALY 145
  DONATELLO OF FLORENCE 147
  THE DELLA ROBBIAS 148
  VERROCCHIO, PUPIL OF DONATELLO 148
  THE GREAT MICHELANGELO 149
  CELLINI AND DA BOLOGNA 151
THE BAROQUE IN SCULPTURE 152
SCULPTURE IN FRANCE 153
NEOCLASSICISM IN SCULPTURE 154
THE 19TH CENTURY 155
SCULPTURE IN THE UNITED STATES 156
     DANIEL CHESTER FRENCH 158
MODERN MOVEMENT 160
  FIGURATIVE AND BIOMORPHIC
  SCULPTURE 162
  THE CONSTRUCTIVIST TRADITION 164
  OBJECTS AND ASSEMBLAGE 166
POSTWAR SCULPTURE 167
     ISAMU NOGUCHI 169
     CHRISTO AND JEANNE-CLAUDE 174

CONCLUSION 179
GLOSSARY 182
BIBLIOGRAPHY 186
INDEX 194

INTRODUCTION

A rt is a means of organizing experience into ordered form. The experience thus translated into a sculpture, song, painting, or poem can then come to life again in the consciousness of other people. It may truly be said that only when this sharing takes place has a work of art been fully realized. That is why art is properly regarded as a language.

To understand the artist's language, however, requires a little effort. Looking at a work of art, like listening to music, becomes a rewarding experience only if the senses are alert to the qualities of the work and to the artist's purpose that brought them into being. The language of sculpture, then, must be learned.

Sculpture, like other arts, is a record of human experience. From earliest times to our own day, sculpture records experiences that range from wars and worship to the simplest joys of seeing and touching suspended shapes designed to move in the wind. In sculpture there is everything from the marble gods of Phidias to the mobiles by Alexander Calder. People everywhere have found the need for sculpture, whether it be in work, in play, or in prayer. Sculpture also records the desire to commemorate the deeds of nations and of individuals.

The Burghers of Calais, a sculpture by Auguste Rodin, is a monument to a historic moment of French dignity and courage. The moment expressed through the six figures is one of trial and triumph. The year depicted

Auguste Rodin depicted a poignant moment during the Hundred Years' War in *The Burghers of Calais* (1889). The tragic yet heroic six figures, executed in bronze, now are located near the Calais town hall.

in the masterpiece was 1347; the place, outside the gates of Calais, was a heavily invaded port town. The English, led by their king, Edward III, had laid siege to the town and starved it into submission. The terms for surrender required that six men come with halters about their necks to deliver the keys of the town.

The fate of these men was clear. They were to pay the penalty for resistance, but in delivering themselves as hostages they would assure safety for the rest of the town.

It was to the memory of the man who volunteered first, Eustache de St-Pierre, the richest burgher of the town, that in 1884 the grateful people of Calais ordered a statue. In working out the idea, however, Rodin was so moved by the incident that he decided to add the five men who volunteered to accompany the leader. Four years after beginning this work, Rodin had given form to his idea and had finally cast it in bronze.

Rodin gives St-Pierre determination and poise. He holds the key to the city, and around his neck is the rope, or halter, prescribed by the conquerors. A companion, with his head buried in his hands, is on the right. These two men exemplify the greatest contrast of feeling in the group. By placing them together Rodin achieves dramatic power. To organize, or compose, six different figures into a single unified work of art, Rodin groups them into three pairs, each pair differing from the other and yet tied to the others in rhythmic movement. The spaces between the figures are also varied. This is what sculpture tries to achieve, for sculpture deals essentially with the purposeful relationships of volumes in space.

By looking at the details of the sculpture one can see Rodin's ability to convey feeling through facial expression and through hands. He cuts the hollows of the face deeply to assure strong shadows, and his textured surfaces catch the subtle variations of light and heighten the sense of life and movement. This irregular surface is a departure from the cold, impersonal smoothness of the classical tradition. Together with a profound sense of power and drama, it had a tremendous influence on the sculptors of Rodin's time and helped to determine the trend of modern sculpture.

While working on a statue, the sculptor relies on proper light to study the planes by which masses turn from the light into the shade, creating the sense of solidity and third dimension. Only by light properly cast can the sculptor study shape, texture, and character.

The sculptor strives to show the finished work in the same light by which it was originally sculpted. A light cast too weakly or too strongly from a source too high or too low can completely change the appearance of the work. It can undo the effort of the sculptor and destroy the effectiveness of the creation.

Paintings too depend on light but not in the same sense as sculpture. The painter asks only that the whole surface of the picture receive uniform and sufficient light for proper viewing. The light and shade used on a face or figure to give it roundness and solidity cannot be altered by an external light. In sculpture, on the other hand, volume and character are brought to life only through light and can be altered at will by the control of light. Proper lighting at night of a statue outdoors also requires skill.

Sculpture differs from painting in another significant respect. A painting, being flat, can show only the view taken by the painter. A statue in full round can be seen from a variety of angles. Consequently the sculptor strives to achieve sense and rhythm for every possible point of view. Sculpture is thus endowed with a variety of interest impossible in painting.

Sculpture by definition, then, is an artistic form in which hard or plastic materials are worked into three-dimensional art objects. The designs may be embodied in freestanding objects, in reliefs on surfaces, or in environments ranging from tableaux to contexts that envelop the spectator. An enormous variety of media may be used, including clay, wax, stone, metal, fabric, glass, wood, plaster, rubber, and random "found" objects. Materials may be carved, modeled, molded, cast, wrought, welded, sewn, assembled, or otherwise shaped and combined.

Sculpture is not a fixed term that applies to a permanently circumscribed category of objects or sets of activities. It is, rather, the name of an art that grows and changes and is continually extending the range of its activities and evolving new kinds of objects. The scope of the term was much wider in the second half of the 20th century than it had been only two or three decades before, and in the fluid state of the visual arts at the turn of the 21st century nobody can predict what its future extensions are likely to be.

Certain features that in previous centuries were considered essential to the art of sculpture are not present in a great deal of modern sculpture and can no longer form part of its definition. One of the most important of these is representation. Before the 20th century, sculpture was considered a representational art, one that imitated forms in life, most often human figures but also inanimate objects, such as game, utensils, and books. Since the turn of the 20th century, however, sculpture had also included nonrepresentational forms. It had long been accepted that the forms of such functional three-dimensional objects as furniture, pots, and buildings may be expressive and beautiful without being in any way representational, but it was only in the 20th century that nonfunctional, nonrepresentational, three-dimensional works of art began to be produced.

Before the 20th century, sculpture was considered primarily an art of solid form, or mass. It is true that the negative elements of sculpture—the voids and hollows within and between its solid forms—have always been to some extent an integral part of its design, but their role was a secondary one. In a great deal of modern sculpture, however, the focus of attention has shifted, and the spatial aspects have become dominant. Spatial sculpture is now a generally accepted branch of the art of sculpture.

It was also taken for granted in the sculpture of the past that its components were of a constant shape and size and, with the exception of items such as Augustus Saint-Gaudens's *Diana* (a monumental weather vane), did not move. With the relatively recent development of kinetic sculpture, neither the immobility nor immutability of its form can any longer be considered essential to the art of sculpture.

Finally, sculpture since the 20th century has not been confined to the two traditional forming processes of carving and modeling or to such traditional natural materials as stone, metal, wood, ivory, bone, and clay. Because present-day sculptors use any materials and methods of manufacture that will serve their purposes, the art of sculpture can no longer be identified with any special materials or techniques.

Through all these changes, there is probably only one thing that has remained constant in the art of sculpture, and it is this that emerges as the central and abiding concern of sculptors: the art of sculpture is the branch of the visual arts that is especially concerned with the creation of form in three dimensions.

Sculpture may be either in the round or in relief. A sculpture in the round is a separate, detached object in its own right, leading the same kind of independent existence in space as a human body or a chair. A relief does not have this kind of independence. It projects from and is attached to or is an integral part of something else that serves either as a background against which it is set or a matrix from which it emerges.

The actual three-dimensionality of sculpture in the round limits its scope in certain respects in comparison with the scope of painting. Sculpture cannot conjure the illusion of space by purely optical means or invest its forms with atmosphere and light as painting can. It does have a kind of reality, a vivid physical presence that is denied to the pictorial arts. The forms of sculpture are tangible as well as visible, and they can appeal strongly and directly to both tactile and visual sensibilities. Even the visually impaired,

including those who are congenitally blind, can produce and appreciate certain kinds of sculpture. It
was, in fact, argued by the 20th-century art critic Sir
Herbert Read that sculpture should be regarded as
primarily an art of touch and that the roots of sculptural sensibility can be traced to the pleasure one
experiences in fondling things.

All three-dimensional forms are perceived as
having an expressive character as well as purely
geometric properties. They strike the observer as
delicate, aggressive, flowing, taut, relaxed, dynamic,
soft, and so on. By exploiting the expressive qualities
of form, a sculptor is able to create images in which
subject matter and expressiveness of form are mutu-
ally reinforcing. Such images go beyond the mere
presentation of fact and communicate a wide range
of subtle and powerful feelings.

The aesthetic raw material of sculpture is, so to
speak, the whole realm of expressive three-dimensional
form. A sculpture may draw upon what already exists in
the endless variety of natural and man-made form, or
it may be an art of pure invention. It has been used to
express a vast range of human emotions and feelings
from the most tender and delicate to the most violent
and ecstatic.

All human beings, intimately involved from birth
with the world of three-dimensional form, learn something of its structural and expressive properties and
develop emotional responses to them. This combination of understanding and sensitive response, often
called a sense of form, can be cultivated and refined.
It is to this sense of form that the art of sculpture primarily appeals. In this comprehensive study, readers

consider the materials, tools, methods, styles, and practices involved in sculpting and many of the techniques that have been used by accomplished artists who have substantially contributed to sculpture as a creative and fine art.

CHAPTER ONE

THE ELEMENTS AND PRINCIPLES OF SCULPTURAL DESIGN

The two most important elements of sculpture—mass and space—are, of course, separable only in thought. All sculpture is made of a material substance that has mass and exists in three-dimensional space. The mass of sculpture is thus the solid, material, space-occupying bulk that is contained within its surfaces. Space enters into the design of sculpture in three main ways: the material components of the sculpture extend into or move through space; they may enclose or enfold space, thus creating hollows and voids within the sculpture; and they may relate one to another across space. Volume, surface, light and shade, and colour are supporting elements of sculpture.

ELEMENTS OF DESIGN

The amount of importance attached to either mass or space in the design of sculpture varies considerably. In Egyptian sculpture and in most of the sculpture of the 20th-century artist Constantin Brancusi, for

Antoine Pevsner's *Construction in Space and in the Third and Fourth Dimensions* (c. 1959–62), in The Hague, uses twisting bronze panels with linear ridges to give a sense of movement in space and time.

example, mass is paramount, and most of the sculptor's thought was devoted to shaping a lump of solid material. In 20th-century works by Antoine Pevsner or Naum Gabo, on the other hand, mass is reduced to a minimum, consisting only of transparent sheets of plastic or thin metal rods. The solid form of the components themselves is of little importance; their main function is to create movement through space and to enclose space. In works by such 20th-century sculptors as Henry Moore and Barbara Hepworth, the elements of space and mass are treated as more or less equal partners.

It is not possible to see the whole of a fully three-dimensional form at once. The observer can only see the whole of it if he turns it around or goes around it himself. For this reason it is sometimes mistakenly assumed that sculpture must be designed primarily to present a series of satisfactory projective views and that this multiplicity of views constitutes the main difference between sculpture and the pictorial arts, which present only one view of their subject. Such an attitude toward sculpture ignores the fact that it is possible to apprehend solid forms as volumes, to conceive an idea of them in the round from any one aspect. A great deal of sculpture is designed to be apprehended primarily as volume.

A single volume is the fundamental unit of three-dimensional solid form that can be conceived in the round. Some sculptures consist of only one volume; others are configurations of a number of volumes. The human figure is often treated by sculptors as a configuration of volumes, each of which corresponds to a major part of the body, such as the head, neck, thorax, and thigh.

Holes and cavities in sculpture, which are as carefully shaped as the solid forms and are of equal importance to the overall design, are sometimes referred to as negative volumes.

The surfaces of sculpture are in fact all that one actually sees. It is from their inflections that one makes inferences about the internal structure of the sculpture. A surface has, so to speak, two aspects: it contains and defines the internal structure of the masses of the sculpture, and it is the part of the sculpture that enters into relations with external space.

The expressive character of different kinds of surfaces is of the utmost importance in sculpture. Double-curved convex surfaces suggest fullness, containment, enclosure, and the outward pressure of internal forces. In the aesthetics of Indian sculpture such surfaces have a special metaphysical significance. Representing the encroachment of space into the mass of the sculpture, concave surfaces suggest the action of external forces and are often indicative of collapse or erosion. Flat surfaces tend to convey a feeling of material hardness and rigidity; they are unbending or unyielding, unaffected by either internal or external pressures. Surfaces that are convex in one curvature and concave in the other can suggest the operation of internal pressures and at the same time a receptivity to the influence of external forces. They are associated with growth, with expansion into space.

Unlike the painter, who creates light effects within the work, the sculptor manipulates actual light on the work. The distribution of light and shade over the forms of his work depends upon the direction and intensity of light from external sources. Nevertheless, to some extent he can determine the kinds of effect this external light will have. If he knows where the work is to be sited, he can adapt it to the kind of light it is likely to receive. The brilliant overhead sunlight of Egypt and India demands a different treatment from the dim interior light of a northern medieval cathedral. Then again, it is possible to create effects of light and shade, or chiaroscuro, by cutting or modeling deep, shadow-catching hollows and prominent, high-lighted ridges. Many late-Gothic sculptors used light and shade as a powerful expressive feature of their work, aiming at a mysterious obscurity, with forms broken by shadow emerging from a dark background. Greek, Indian, and most Italian Renaissance sculptors shaped the forms of their work to receive light in a way that makes the whole work radiantly clear.

The colouring of sculpture may be either natural or applied. In the recent past, sculptors became more aware than ever before of the inherent beauty of sculptural materials. Under the slogan of "truth to materials" many of them worked their materials in ways that exploited their natural properties, including colour and texture. More recently, however, there has been a growing tendency to use bright artificial colouring as an important element in the design of sculpture.

In the ancient world and during the Middle Ages almost all sculpture was artificially coloured, usually in a bold and decorative rather than a naturalistic manner. The sculptured portal of a cathedral, for example, would be coloured and gilded with all the

The carved stone figures on the portal and façade of the Gothic Chartres Cathedral, France, were once coloured and gilded, as most exterior sculptures were in the Middle Ages.

brilliance of a contemporary illuminated manuscript. Combinations of differently coloured materials, such as the ivory and gold of some Greek sculpture, were not unknown before the 17th century, but the early Baroque sculptor Gian Lorenzo Bernini greatly extended the practice by combining variously coloured marbles with white marble and gilt bronze.

PRINCIPLES OF DESIGN

It is doubtful whether any principles of design are universal in the art of sculpture, for the principles that govern the organization of the elements of sculpture into expressive compositions differ from style to style. In fact, distinctions made among the major styles of sculpture are largely based on a recognition of differences in the principles of design that underlie them. Thus, the art historian Erwin Panofsky was attempting to define a difference of principle in the design of Romanesque and Gothic sculpture when he stated that the forms of Romanesque were conceived as projections from a plane outside themselves, while those of Gothic were conceived as being centred on an axis within themselves. The "principle of axiality" was considered by Panofsky to be "the essential principle of classical statuary," which Gothic had rediscovered.

The principles of sculptural design govern the approaches of sculptors to such fundamental matters as orientation, proportion, scale, articulation, and balance.

For conceiving and describing the orientation of the forms of sculpture in relation to each other, to a spectator, and to their surroundings, some kind of spatial scheme of reference is required. This is provided by a system of axes and planes of reference.

An axis is an imaginary centre line through a symmetrical or near symmetrical volume or group of volumes that suggests the gravitational pivot of the mass. Thus, all the main components of the human body have axes of their own, while an upright figure has a single vertical axis running through its entire length. Volumes may rotate or tilt on their axes.

Planes of reference are imaginary planes to which the movements, positions, and directions of volumes, axes, and surfaces may be referred. The principal planes of reference are the frontal, the horizontal, and the two profile planes.

Hermes Carrying the Infant Dionysus (c. 350–330 BCE) by Praxiteles (or a Hellenistic copy) has the figure Hermes displaying a contrapposto pose.

The principles that govern the characteristic poses and spatial compositions of upright figures in different styles of sculpture are formulated with reference to axes and the four cardinal planes: for example, the principle of axiality already referred to; the principle of frontality, which governs the design of Archaic sculpture; the characteristic contrapposto (pose in which parts of the body, such as upper and lower, tilt or even twist in opposite directions) of Michelangelo's figures; and in standing Greek sculpture of the Classical period the frequently used balanced "chiastic" pose (stance in which the body weight is taken principally on one leg, thereby creating a contrast of tension and relaxation between the opposite sides of a figure).

Proportional relations exist among linear dimensions, areas, and volumes and masses. All three types of proportion coexist and interact in sculpture, contributing to its expressiveness and beauty. Attitudes toward proportion differ considerably among sculptors. Some sculptors, both abstract

CONTRAPPOSTO

Contrapposto (Italian: "opposite"), in the visual arts, is a sculptural scheme, originated by the ancient Greeks, in which the standing human figure is poised such that the weight rests on one leg (called the engaged leg), freeing the other leg, which is bent at the knee. With the weight shift, the hips, shoulders, and head tilt, suggesting relaxation with the subtle internal organic movement that denotes life. Contrapposto may be used for draped as well as nude figures. The Greeks invented this formula in the early 5th century BCE as an alternative to the stiffly static pose–in which the weight is distributed equally on both legs–that had dominated Greek figure sculpture in earlier periods. There is a clear development from the *Critius Boy* of the 5th century, whose leg is bent while his torso remains erect, to the completely relaxed 4th-century *Hermes Carrying the Infant Dionysus* by Praxiteles. The rhythmic ease of the contrapposto pose vastly enlarged the expressive possibilities of figure sculpture.

Gothic sculpture occasionally retained the idea of a supporting and a bent leg, transforming it so that the figure appeared to rise from, rather than rest heavily upon, the ground.

(CONTINUED ON THE NEXT PAGE)

(CONTINUED FROM THE PREVIOUS PAGE)

Italian Renaissance artists such as Donatello and Andrea del Verrocchio revived the classical formula, giving it the name contrapposto, which suggests the action and reaction of the various parts of the figure, and enriching the conception by scientific anatomical study. Michelangelo introduced a tension of masses by pushing one forward and another back—thrusting an arm forward over a receding leg, for instance. The *David*, which exemplifies his method, deeply influenced Gian Lorenzo Bernini and other Baroque sculptors. In modern times, contrapposto has been used for naturalistic representations of the relaxed standing figure, as in Aristide Maillol's *Venus with a Necklace* (c. 1918–28).

and figurative, use mathematical systems of proportion; for example, the refinement and idealization of natural human proportions was a major preoccupation of Greek sculptors. Indian sculptors employed iconometric canons, or systems of carefully related proportions, that determined the proportions of all significant dimensions of the human figure. African and other tribal sculptors base the proportions of their figures on the subjective importance of the parts of the body. Unnatural proportions may be used for expressive purposes or to accommodate a sculpture to its surroundings. The elongation of the figures on the Portail Royal ("Royal Portal") of Chartres Cathedral does both: it enhances

The Portail Royal of Chartres Cathedral contains stone figures (1145–50) that were elongated by the sculptor to add to their spiritual character but also to incorporate them into the columnar structure of the doorway.

their otherworldliness and also integrates them with the columnar architecture.

Sometimes it is necessary to adapt the proportions of sculpture to suit its position in relation to a viewer. A figure sited high on a building, for example, is usually made larger in its upper parts in order to counteract the effects of foreshortening. This should be allowed for when a sculpture intended for such a position is exhibited on eye level in a museum.

The scale of sculpture must sometimes be considered in relation to the scale of its surroundings. When it is one element in a larger complex, such as the facade of a building, it must be in scale with the rest. Another important consideration that sculptors must take into account when designing outdoor sculpture is the tendency of sculpture in the open air—particularly when viewed against the sky—to appear less massive than it does in a studio. Because one tends to relate the scale of sculpture to one's own human physical dimensions, the emotional impact of a colossal figure and a small figurine are quite different.

In ancient and medieval sculpture the relative scale of the figures in a composition is often determined by their importance, e.g., slaves are much smaller than kings or nobles. This is sometimes known as hierarchic scale.

The joining of one form to another may be accomplished in a variety of ways. In much of the work of the 19th-century French sculptor Auguste Rodin, there are no clear boundaries, and one form is merged with another in an impressionistic manner to create a continuously flowing surface. In works by the Greek sculptor Praxiteles, the forms are softly and subtly blended by means of smooth, blurred transitions. The volumes of Indian sculpture and the surface anatomy of male figures in the style of the Greek sculptor Polyclitus are sharply defined and clearly

FORESHORTENING

Foreshortening is the method of rendering a specific object or figure in a picture in depth.

The artist records, in varying degrees, the distortion that is seen by the eye when an object or figure is viewed at a distance or at an unusual angle. In a photograph of a recumbent figure positioned so that the feet are nearest the camera, for instance, the feet will seem unnaturally large and those body parts at a distance, such as the head, unnaturally small. The artist may either record this effect exactly, producing a startling illusion of reality that seems to violate the picture plane (surface of the picture), or modify it, slightly reducing the relative size of the nearer part of the object, so as to make a less-aggressive assault on the viewer's eye and to relate the foreshortened object more harmoniously to the rest of the picture.

Insofar as foreshortening is basically concerned with the persuasive projection of a form in an illusionistic way, it is a type of perspective, but the term *foreshortening* is almost invariably used in relation to a single object, or part of an object, rather than to a scene or group of objects.

articulated. One of the main distinctions between the work of Italian and northern Renaissance sculptors lies in the Italians' preference for compositions made up of clearly articulated, distinct units of form and the tendency of the northern Europeans to subordinate the individual parts to the allover flow of the composition.

The balance, or equilibrium, of freestanding sculpture has three aspects. First, the sculpture must have actual physical stability. This can be achieved by natural balance—that is, by making the sculpture stable enough in itself to stand firmly—which is easy enough to do with a four-legged animal or a reclining figure but not with a standing figure or a tall, thin sculpture, which must be secured to a base. The second aspect of balance is compositional. The interaction of forces and the distribution of weight within a composition may produce a state of either dynamic or static equilibrium. The third aspect of balance applies only to sculpture that represents a living figure. A live human figure balances on two feet by making constant move-ments and muscular adjustments. Such an effect can be conveyed in sculpture by subtle displacements of form and suggestions of tension and relaxation.

RELATIONSHIPS TO OTHER ARTS

Sculpture has long been closely related to architecture through its role as architectural decoration and also at the level of design. Architecture, like sculpture, is con-cerned with three-dimensional form, and, although the central problem in the design of buildings is the orga-nization of space rather than mass, there are styles of architecture that are effective largely through the quality

Gian Lorenzo Bernini's marble and gilded bronze niche sculpture *The Ecstasy of St. Teresa* (1645–52) is in Santa Maria della Vittoria in Rome. It depicts the mystical experience of Teresa of Ávila and stands as Bernini's ideal of a three-dimensional picture.

and organization of their solid forms. Ancient styles of stone architecture, particularly Egyptian, Greek, and Mexican, tend to treat their components in a sculptural manner. Moreover, most buildings viewed from the outside are compositions of masses. The growth of spatial sculpture is so intimately related to the opening up and lightening of architecture, which the development of modern building technology has made possible, that many 20th- and 21st-century sculptors can be said to have treated their work in an architectural manner.

Some forms of relief sculpture approach very closely the pictorial arts of painting, drawing, engraving, and so on. And sculptures in the round that make use of chiaroscuro and that are conceived primarily as pictorial views rather than as compositions in the round are said to be "painterly," for example, Bernini's *Ecstasy of St. Teresa* (Santa Maria della Vittoria, Rome).

The borderlines between sculpture and pottery and the metalworking arts are not clear-cut, and many pottery and metal artifacts have every claim to be considered as sculpture. Today there is a growing affinity between the work of industrial designers and sculptors. Sculptural modeling techniques, and sometimes sculptors themselves, are often involved, for example, in the initial stages of the design of new automobile bodies.

The close relationships that exist between sculpture and the other visual arts are attested by the number of artists who have readily turned from one art to another, for example, Michelangelo, Bernini, Pisanello, Degas, and Picasso.

CHAPTER TWO

MATERIALS OF SCULPTURE AND THEIR CONSERVATION AND REPAIR

A ny material that can be shaped in three dimensions can be used sculpturally. Certain materials, by virtue of their structural and aesthetic properties and their availability, have proved especially suitable. The most important of these are stone, wood, metal, clay, ivory, and plaster. There are also a number of materials of secondary importance and many that have only recently come into use.

PRIMARY

Throughout history, stone has been the principal material of monumental sculpture. There are practical reasons for this: many types of stone are highly resistant to the weather and therefore suitable for external use; stone is available in all parts of the world and can be obtained in large blocks; many stones have a fairly homogeneous texture and a uniform hardness that make them suitable for carving; stone has been the chief material used for the monumental architecture with which so much sculpture has been associated.

Stones belonging to all three main categories of rock formation have been used in sculpture. Igneous rocks, which are formed by the cooling of molten masses of mineral as they approach the earth's surface, include granite, diorite, basalt, and obsidian. These are some of the hardest stones used for sculpture. Sedimentary rocks, which include sandstones and limestones, are formed from accumulated deposits of mineral and organic substances. Sandstones are agglomerations of particles of eroded stone held together by a cementing substance. Limestones are formed chiefly from the calcareous remains of organisms. Alabaster (gypsum), also a sedimentary rock, is a chemical deposit. Many varieties of sandstone and limestone, which vary greatly in quality and suitability for carving, are used for sculpture. Because of their method of formation, many sedimentary rocks have pronounced strata and are rich in fossils.

Metamorphic rocks result from changes brought about in the structure of sedimentary and igneous rocks by extreme pressure or heat. The most well-known metamorphic rocks used in sculpture are the marbles, which are recrystallized limestones. Italian Carrara marble, the best known, was used by Roman and Renaissance sculptors, especially Michelangelo, and is still widely used. The best-known varieties used by Greek sculptors, with whom marble was more popular than any other stone, are Pentelic—from which the Parthenon and its sculpture are made—and Parian.

Because stone is extremely heavy and lacks tensile strength, it is easily fractured if carved too thinly and not properly supported. A massive treatment without vulnerable projections, as in Egyptian and pre-Columbian American Indian sculpture, is therefore usually

Michelangelo sculpted the *Pietà* (1499), located in St. Peter's Basilica, Rome, from a block of Carrara marble. This pietà represents the Virgin Mary mourning and holding the dead body of Christ.

MARBLE

Sculptors and architects for centuries have used the beautiful and strong stone called marble for their work. Composed largely of calcite (a form of calcium carbonate), marble is a metamorphic rock that forms when limestone is recrystallized under the influence of heat, pressure, and chemical processes beneath Earth's surface.

Marble forms from limestone, a sedimentary rock rich in calcium carbonate. This carbonate comes from the skeletons and shells of marine organisms such as foraminiferans. When these organisms died millions of years ago, their mineral remains sank to the ocean floor, forming layers of sediment. Over time these layers were buried by mud and other sediments that pressed and cemented them into limestone. Water, heat, and pressure then metamorphosed, or changed, the rock into marble. As marble the rock is more compact and crystalline. Some forms of marble metamorphosed from dolomite, a type of limestone composed of calcium magnesium carbonate. The formation of limestone and its metamorphosis into marble are part of a natural process called the rock cycle.

Commercially, any rock containing calcium carbonate that can be polished is called marble. The so-called onyx marbles did not metamorphose from limestone but are calcium carbonate deposited by water. Verd antiques are marbles made up chiefly of serpentine, a hydrous magnesium silicate.

True marble varies widely in color, from white to black through almost every shade of the spectrum. Impurities such as silica, iron oxides, and graphite give marble its color and characteristic rich veining and clouding. Pure marble is white. The texture of marble ranges widely from fine to coarse, and it takes a good polish.

Marble is very durable and generally does not absorb much water. Nonporous marble with uniform grain size is highly resistant to moisture and fire, making it ideal for monuments and fireproof buildings. Architects use it for columns, walls, floors, and steps, both interior and exterior. Interior designers also use it to decorate such items as tabletops and fireplaces.

Because marble is composed largely of calcium carbonate, it reacts with acids. This chemical reaction changes the calcium carbonate in the rock to soluble salts that are washed away. Moist air and rain are slightly acidic because they contain atmospheric

(CONTINUED ON THE NEXT PAGE)

(*CONTINUED FROM THE PREVIOUS PAGE*)

gases such as carbon dioxide and sulfur dioxide that have a low pH. Marble exposed to atmospheric moisture and rain is thus degraded, or worn away, by these substances.

Phidias sculpted this metope from Pentelic marble (c. 447–438 BCE) for the Parthenon in Athens, Greece.

This process, known as weathering, is more pronounced when marble is exposed to acid rain, which contains a higher concentration of acidic gases.

Marble is highly prized not only for its beauty but also for the relative ease in carving and shaping it. The ancient Greeks used Parian marble from the Island of Paros for such famous statues as the *Venus de Milo*. They built the Parthenon in Athens of Pentelic marble from Mount Pentelicus. The Taj Mahal is covered in pure white Makrana marble. The Lincoln Memorial in Washington, D.C., is made from several American marbles. Pure white marble from Carrara, Italy, was used by the Romans and such Renaissance sculptors as Michelangelo and Antonio Canova. It is still favored by modern sculptors.

Marble is found in many places. Italy, Spain, Brazil, China, India, Portugal, and Turkey are among the world's top producers of marble, with each country quarrying more than one million tons each year. The United States produces many types of marble. Historically marble was quarried in a number of U.S. states, including Missouri, Colorado, and Alabama. Today, Vermont, Tennessee, and Georgia lead in quarrying marble as dimension stone (blocks or slabs) for buildings and monuments.

preferred. Some stones, however, can be treated more freely and openly; marble in particular has been treated by some European sculptors with almost the same freedom as bronze, but such displays of virtuosity are achieved by overcoming rather than submitting to the properties of the material itself.

The colours and textures of stone are among its most delightful properties. Some stones are fine-grained and can be carved with delicate detail and finished with a high polish; others are coarse-grained and demand a broader treatment. Pure white Carrara marble, which has a translucent quality, seems to glow and responds to light in a delicate, subtle manner. (These properties of marble were brilliantly exploited by 15th-century Italian sculptors such as Donatello and Desiderio da Settignano.) The colouring of granite is not uniform but has a salt-and-pepper quality and may glint with mica and quartz crystals. It may be predominantly black or white or a variety of grays, pinks, and reds. Sandstones vary in texture and are often warmly coloured in a range of buffs, pinks, and reds. Limestones vary greatly in colour, and the presence of fossils may add to the interest of their surfaces. A number of stones are richly variegated in colour by the irregular veining that runs through them.

Hardstones, or semiprecious stones, constitute a special group, which includes

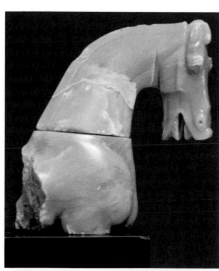

A Chinese sculpture in jade from the Han dynasty (206 BCE–220 CE) depicts a horse's head.

some of the most beautiful and decorative of all substances. The working of these stones, along with the working of more precious gemstones, is usually considered as part of the glyptic (gem carving or engraving), or lapidary, arts, but many artifacts produced from them can be considered small-scale sculpture. They are often harder to work than steel. First among the hardstones used for sculpture is jade, which was venerated by the ancient Chinese, who worked it, together with other hardstones, with extreme skill. It was also used sculpturally by Maya and Mexican artists. Other important hardstones are rock crystal, rose quartz, amethyst, agate, and jasper.

The principal material of tribal sculpture in Africa, Oceania, and North America, wood has also been used by every great civilization; it was used extensively during the Middle Ages, for example, especially in Germany and central Europe. Among modern sculptors who have used wood for important works are Ernst Barlach, Ossip Zadkine, and Henry Moore.

Both hardwoods and softwoods are used for sculpture. Some are close-grained, and they cut like cheese; others are open-grained and stringy. The fibrous structure of wood gives it considerable tensile strength so that it may be carved thinly and with greater freedom than stone. For large or complex open compositions, a number of pieces of wood may be jointed. Wood is used mainly for indoor sculpture, for it is not as tough or durable as stone; changes of humidity and temperature may cause it to split, and it is subject to attack by insects and fungus. The grain of wood is one of its most attractive features, giving variety of pattern and texture to its surfaces. Its colours, too, are subtle and varied. In general, wood has a warmth that stone does not have, but it lacks the massive dignity and weight of stone.

The principal woods for sculpture are oak, mahogany, limewood, walnut, elm, pine, cedar, boxwood, pear, and ebony, but many others are also used. The sizes of wood available are limited by the sizes of trees; North American Indians, for example, could carve gigantic totem poles in pine, but boxwood is available only in small pieces.

In the 20th century, wood was used by many sculptors as a medium for construction as well as for carving. Laminated timbers, chipboards, and timber in block and plank form can be glued, jointed, screwed, or bolted together and given a variety of finishes.

Wherever metal technologies have been developed, metals have been used for sculpture. The amount of metal sculpture that has survived from the ancient world does not properly reflect the extent to which it was used, for vast quantities have been plundered and melted down. Countless Far Eastern and Greek metal sculptures have been lost in this way, as has almost all the goldwork of pre-Columbian American Indians.

The metal most used for sculpture is bronze, which is basically an alloy of copper and tin, but gold, silver, aluminum, copper, brass, lead, and iron have also been widely used. Most metals are extremely strong, hard, and durable, with a tensile strength that permits a much greater freedom of design than is possible in either stone or wood. A life-size bronze figure that is firmly attached to a base needs no support other than its own feet and may even be poised on one foot. Considerable attenuation of form is also possible without risk of fracture.

The colour, brilliant lustre, and reflectivity of metal surfaces have been highly valued and made full use of in sculpture although, since the Renaissance, artificial patinas have generally been preferred as finishes for bronze.

Metals can be worked in a variety of ways in order to produce sculpture. They can be cast—that is, melted and poured into molds; squeezed under pressure into dies, as in coin making; or worked directly—for example, by hammering, bending, cutting, welding, and repoussé (hammered or pressed in relief).

Important traditions of bronze sculpture are Greek, Roman, Indian (especially Chola), African (Bini and Yoruba), Italian Renaissance, and Chinese. Gold was used to great effect for small-scale works in pre-Columbian America and medieval Europe. A fairly recent discovery, aluminum has been used a great deal by modern sculptors. Iron has not been used much as a casting material, but in recent years it has become a popular material for direct working by techniques similar to those of the blacksmith. Sheet metal is one of the principal materials used nowadays for constructional sculpture. Stainless steel in sheet form has been used effectively by the American sculptor David Smith.

Clay is one of the most common and easily obtainable of all materials. Used for modeling animal and human figures long before men discovered how to fire pots, it has been one of the sculptor's chief materials ever since.

Clay has four properties that account for its widespread use: when moist, it is one of the most plastic of all substances, easily modeled and capable of registering the most detailed impressions; when partially

DAVID SMITH

David Smith (1906–65) was an American sculptor whose pioneering welded metal sculpture and massive painted geometric forms made him the most original American sculptor in the decades after World War II. His work greatly influenced the brightly coloured "primary structures" of Minimal art during the 1960s.

Smith was never trained as a sculptor, but he learned to work with metal in 1925, when he was briefly employed as a riveter at the Studebaker automobile plant in South Bend, Indiana. Dropping out of college after his first year, he moved to New York City and, while working variously as a taxi driver, salesman, and carpenter, studied painting under John Sloan and the Czech abstract painter Jan Matulka.

Smith's sculpture grew out of his early abstract paintings of urban scenes, which were reminiscent of the work of his friend Stuart Davis. Experimenting with texture, he began to attach bits of wood, metal strips, and found objects to his paintings, until the canvases were reduced to virtual bases supporting sculptural superstructures. Long after he stopped painting, his sculpture continued to betray its pictorial origins: his overriding concern with the interplay of two-dimensional planes and the articulation of their surfaces led Smith to abrade or to paint his sculpture while often ignoring the traditional sculptural problems of developing forms in three-dimensional space.

Smith's interest in freestanding sculpture dates from the early 1930s, when he first saw illustrations of the welded metal sculpture of Pablo Picasso and another Spanish sculptor, Julio González. Following their example, Smith became the first American artist to make welded metal sculpture. He found a creative freedom in this technique that, combined with the liberating influence of the Surrealist doctrine that art springs from the spontaneous expression of the unconscious mind, allowed him soon to produce a large body of abstract biomorphic forms remarkable for their erratic inventiveness, their stylistic diversity, and their high aesthetic quality.

In 1940 Smith moved to Bolton Landing, New York, where he made sculpture during World War II when not assembling locomotives and tanks in a defense plant. For a time

(CONTINUED ON THE NEXT PAGE)

(*CONTINUED FROM THE PREVIOUS PAGE*)

after the war, he continued to work in a bewildering profusion of styles, but toward the end of the decade he disciplined his exuberant imagination by making pieces in stylistically unified series. Such series of sculptures were often continued over a period of years concurrently with other series of radically different styles. With the *Albany* series (begun in 1959) and the *Zig* series the following year, Smith's work became more geometric and monumental. In *Zigs*, his most successful Cubist works, he used paint to emphasize the relationships of planes, but in his *Cubi* (begun in 1963), his last great series, Smith relied instead on the light of the sculptures' outdoor surroundings to bring their burnished stainless-steel surfaces to life. These pieces abandon two-dimensional planes for cylinders and rectilinear solids that achieve a sense of massive volume. Smith joined these cubiform elements at odd and seemingly haphazard angles, in dynamically unstable arrangements that communicate an effect of weightlessness and freedom.

dried out to a leather-hard state or completely dried, it can be carved and scraped; when mixed with enough water, it becomes a creamy liquid known as slip, which may be poured into molds and allowed to dry; when fired to temperatures of between 700 and 1,400 °C (1,300 and 2,600 °F), it undergoes irreversible structural changes that make it permanently hard and extremely durable.

Sculptors use clay as a material for working out ideas; for preliminary models that are subsequently cast in such materials as plaster, metal, and concrete or carved in stone; and for pottery sculpture.

Depending on the nature of the clay body itself and the temperature at which it is fired, a finished pottery product is said to be earthenware, which is opaque, relatively soft, and porous; stoneware, which is hard, nonporous, and more or less vitrified; or porcelain, which is fine-textured, vitrified, and translucent. All three types of pottery are used for sculpture. Sculpture made in low-fired clays, particularly buff and red clays, is known as terra-cotta (baked earth). This term is used inconsistently, however, and is often extended to cover all forms of pottery sculpture.

Unglazed clay bodies can be smooth or coarse in texture and may be coloured white, gray, buff, brown, pink, or red. Pottery sculpture can be decorated with any of the techniques invented by potters and coated with a variety of beautiful glazes.

Paleolithic sculptors produced relief and in-the-round work in unfired clay. The ancient Chinese, particularly during the Tang (618–907) and Song (960–1279) dynasties, made superb pottery sculpture, including large-scale human figures. The best-known

TERRA-COTTA

Literally, terra-cotta is any kind of fired clay, but, in general usage, it is a kind of object–e.g., vessel, figure, or structural form–made from fairly coarse, porous clay that when fired assumes a colour ranging from dull ochre to red and usually is left unglazed. Most terra-cotta has been of a utilitarian kind because of its cheapness, versatility, and durability. Limitations in the basic materials often cause a superficial similarity between simply made works as far separated by time and distance as early Greece and the modern cultures of Latin America.

Throughout the ancient world, one of the most common uses of terra-cotta was for building-brick, roof tiles, and sarcophagi, the last often decorated with paintings. Small terra-cotta figures from the Early Bronze Age, as early as 3000 BCE, have been found in Greece, and larger objects dating from the 7th century BCE have also been found. Greek artists carried the craft to Etruria, whence both Etruscan and Greek sculptors moved to work in Rome. Most Greek terra-cotta statuary, more common than once thought, was used to decorate temples. The modeled Etruscan statues, at times very Greek in style but often with a gayer or fiercer flavour, were admired widely in antiquity. Figures on Etruscan sarcophagi often were of terra-cotta. Few Roman terra-cotta statues have been found.

Molded statuettes 6 to 7 inches (15 to 18 cm) in height are common throughout the ancient world, among them very early primitive figures from Cyprus and painted, glazed human figures from Minoan Crete. The Cypriot figures often comprise groups of dancers or warriors, and the Cretan feature lively poses of women, horsemen, or animals. After the 7th century BCE, styles became less hieratic, the subjects more mundane—e.g., a nurse with child, a teacher and pupils, an actor in costume. The Tanagra figurines, found in Tanagra in central Greece (Boeotia), are the best known of this kind. In the Hellenistic period, from the 4th century BCE, centres of statuette production moved to Asia Minor and westward, being found throughout the Roman Empire as far as Britain. Styles in the East became more ornate and influenced by Oriental values in design and subject.

(CONTINUED ON THE NEXT PAGE)

(CONTINUED FROM THE PREVIOUS PAGE)

Architectural relief, especially where wood or clay was used for building, used floral or more abstract designs and such figured representations as chariot races or animal or female heads; examples have been found in Asia Minor, Greece, and Etruscanized southern Italy. Votive reliefs also were common, notably those of the local divinities and heroes rendered broadly and smoothly in Tarentum (Taranto), southern Italy, and the small, meticulous reliefs of local cults found at Locris in central Greece. The fine 5th-century reliefs from the island of Melos, in which mythological scenes predominate, decorated chests. Much Roman architecture is decorated with relief themes from mythology, especially of Dionysus and his revellers.

The use of terra-cotta for all purposes virtually died out between the end of the Roman Empire and the 14th century. In 15th-century Italy and Germany it appeared again, either molded or carved, and in its natural colour as friezes, moldings, or inset medallions decorating buildings. A new use of terra-cotta was in the highly glazed and coloured sculpture introduced in Florence early in the 15th century by the della Robbia family. The effect, adding a freshness of accent especially to marble and stone, was imitated widely, and the use of terra-cotta, glazed or unglazed, spread throughout Europe. Free sculpture in terra-cotta also was revived in the 15th century by such artists as Donatello, Verrocchio, and especially Guido Mazzoni and Antonio Begarelli working in Modena; often it was painted in natural colours or to imitate marble or bronze.

During the following centuries, most terra-cotta figures were executed as preliminary studies, though the works of such 18th-century French artists as Jean-Baptiste Lemoyne and Jean-Antoine Houdon display a personal immediacy of subject that is not transferable to the harder material. In the same period, such pottery centres as Sèvres in France introduced finely wrought small groups with allegorical and mythological themes. Terra-cotta was used both architecturally and for figures during the 19th century, but its modern revival dates from the 20th century, when both potters and architects again became interested in the aesthetic properties of the material.

The Jaina pottery figurine (Late Classic Maya style) pictured here is from Campeche, Mexico.

Greek works are the intimate small-scale figures and groups from Tanagra. Mexican and Maya sculptor-potters produced vigorous, directly modeled figures. During the Renaissance, pottery was used in Italy for major sculptural projects, including the large-scale glazed and coloured sculptures of Luca della Robbia and his family, which are among the finest works in the medium. One of the most popular uses of the pottery medium has been for the manufacture of figurines, at Staffordshire, Meissen, and Sèvres, for example.

The main source of ivory is elephant tusks, but walrus, hippopotamus, narwhal (an Arctic aquatic animal), and, in Paleolithic times, mammoth tusks also were used for sculpture. Ivory is dense, hard, and difficult to work. Its colour is creamy white, which usually yellows with age, and it will take a high polish. A tusk may be sawed into panels for relief carving or into blocks for carving in the round, or the shape of the tusk itself may be used. The physical properties of the material invite the most delicate, detailed carving, and displays of virtuosity are common.

Ivory was used extensively in antiquity in the Middle and Far East and the Mediterranean. An almost unbroken Christian tradition of ivory carving reaches from Rome and Byzantium to the end of the Middle Ages. Throughout this time, ivory was used mainly in relief, often in conjunction with precious metals, enamels, and precious stones to produce the most splendid effects. Some of its main sculptural uses were for devotional diptychs, portable altars, book covers, retables (raised shelves above altars), caskets, and crucifixes. The Baroque period, too, is rich in ivories, especially in Germany. A fine tradition of ivory carving also existed in Benin, a former kingdom of West Africa.

Related to ivory, horn and bone have been used since Paleolithic times for small-scale sculpture. Reindeer horn and walrus tusks were two of the Eskimo carver's most important materials. One of the finest of all medieval "ivories" is a carving in whalebone, *The Adoration of the Magi.*

Plaster of paris (sulfate of lime) is especially useful for the production of molds, casts, and preliminary models. It was used by Egyptian and Greek sculptors as a casting medium and is today the most versatile material in the sculptor's workshop.

When mixed with water, plaster will in a short time recrystallize, or set—that is, become hard and inert—and its volume will increase slightly. When set, it is relatively fragile and lacking in character and is therefore of limited use for finished work. Plaster can be poured as a liquid, modeled directly when of a suitable consistency, or easily carved after it has set. Other materials can be added to it to retard its setting, to increase its hardness or resistance to heat, to change its colour, or to reinforce it.

The main sculptural use of plaster in the past was for molding and casting clay models as a stage in the production of cast metal sculpture. Many sculptors today omit the clay-modeling stage and model directly in plaster. As a mold material in the casting of concrete

PLASTER OF PARIS

Plaster of paris is a quick-setting gypsum plaster consisting of a fine white powder (calcium sulfate hemihydrate), which hardens when moistened and allowed to dry. Known since ancient times, plaster of paris is so called because of its preparation from the abundant gypsum found near Paris.

Plaster of paris does not generally shrink or crack when dry, making it an excellent medium for casting molds. It is commonly used to precast and hold parts of ornamental plasterwork placed on ceilings and cornices. It is also used in medicine to make plaster casts to immobilize broken bones while they heal, though some orthopedic casts are made of fibreglass or thermoplastics. Some sculptors work directly in plaster of paris, as the speed at which the plaster sets gives the work a sense of immediacy and enables the sculptor to achieve the original idea quickly. In medieval and Renaissance times, gesso (usually made of plaster of paris mixed with glue) was applied to wood panels, plaster, stone, or canvas to provide the ground for tempera and oil painting.

Plaster of paris is prepared by heating calcium sulfate dihydrate, or gypsum, to 120–180 °C (248–356 °F). With an additive to retard the set, it is called wall, or hard wall, plaster, which can provide passive fire protection for interior surfaces.

and fibreglass sculpture, plaster is widely used. It has great value as a material for reproducing existing sculpture; many museums, for example, use such casts for study purposes.

SECONDARY

Basically, concrete is a mixture of an aggregate (usually sand and small pieces of stone) bound together by cement. A variety of stones, such as crushed marble, granite chips, and gravel, can be used, each giving a different effect of colour and texture. Commercial cement is gray, white, or black, but it can be coloured by additives. The cement most widely used by sculptors is *ciment fondu*, which is extremely hard and quick setting. A recent invention—at least, in appropriate forms for sculpture—concrete is rapidly replacing stone for certain types of work. Because it is cheap, hard, tough, and durable, it is particularly suitable for large outdoor projects, especially decorative wall surfaces. With proper reinforcement it permits great freedom of design. And by using techniques similar to those of the building industry, sculptors are able to create works in concrete on a gigantic scale.

When synthetic resins, especially polyesters, are reinforced with laminations of glass fibre, the result is a lightweight shell that is extremely strong, hard, and durable. It is usually known simply as fibreglass. After having been successfully used for car bodies, boat hulls, and the like, it has developed recently into an important material for sculpture. Because the material is visually unattractive in itself, it is usually coloured by means of fillers and pigments. It was first used in sculpture in conjunction with powdered metal fillers in order to produce cheap "cold-cast" substitutes for bronze and aluminum, but with the recent tendency to use bright colours in sculpture it is now often coloured either by pigmenting the material itself or by painting.

It is possible to model fibreglass, but more usually it is cast as a laminated shell. Its possibilities for sculpture have not yet been fully exploited.

Various formulas for modeling wax have been used in the past, but these have been generally replaced by synthetic waxes. The main uses of wax in sculpture have been as a preliminary modeling material for metal casting by the lost-wax, or cire-perdue, process and for making sketches. It is not durable enough for use as a material in its own right, although it has been used for small works, such as wax fruit, that can be kept under a glass dome.

Papier-mâché (pulped paper bonded with glue) has been used for sculpture, especially in the Far East. Mainly used for decorative work, especially masks, it can have considerable strength; the Japanese, for example, made armour from it. Sculpture made of sheet paper is a limited art form used only for ephemeral and usually trivial work.

Numerous other permanent materials—such as shells, amber, and brick—and ephemeral ones—such as feathers, baker's dough, sugar, bird seed, foliage, ice and snow, and cake icing—have been used for fashioning three-dimensional images. In view of late 20th-century trends in sculpture it is no longer possible to speak of "the materials of sculpture." Modern sculpture has no special materials. Any material, natural or man-made, is likely to be used, including inflated polyethylene, foam rubber, expanded polystyrene, fabrics,

PAPIER-MÂCHÉ

Papier-mâché (French: "chewed paper") is repulped paper that has been mixed with glue or paste so that it can be molded. The art of making articles of papier-mâché, beautifully decorated in Oriental motifs and handsomely lacquered, was known in the East centuries before its introduction in Europe. Ancient masks of Buddhist deities were made of papier-mâché in Tibet sometime after the 8th century. Since it can be a strong substance, the Japanese made armour from it, and it has been used for sculpture in East Asia. It was mainly used to make beautifully decorated, handsomely lacquered objects.

Molded-paper products were first made in France in the early part of the 18th century and, later, in Germany and England. Different processes were used; for instance, several sheets of paper glued together could be pressure molded into such articles as trays and furniture panels. Although production has declined since the 19th century, papier-mâché is still used for toys, masks, theatre props, model scenic materials, and the like.

Claes Oldenburg's *Giant Hamburger* (1962) is painted sailcloth stuffed with foam rubber. Oldenburg often used unconventional materials for his sculptures.

and neon tubes; the materials for a sculpture by Claes Oldenburg, for example, are listed as canvas, cloth, Dacron, metal, foam rubber, and Plexiglas. Real objects, too, may be incorporated in sculpture, as in the mixed-medium compositions of Edward Kienholz; even junk has its devotees, who fashion "junk" sculpture.

CONSERVATION AND RESTORATION OF SCULPTURE

Art conservation and restoration attempt to conserve and repair architecture, paintings, drawings, prints, sculptures, and objects of the decorative arts (furniture, glassware, metalware, textiles, ceramics, and so on) that have been adversely affected by negligence, willful damage, or more usually, the inevitable decay caused by the effects of time and human use on the materials of which they are made.

Throughout history, artists and craftsmen have created sculpture by using virtually every material imaginable. Stone has been chiseled, metal hammered or cast, wood carved, and clay molded. Bone, ivory, and resins have been shaped with knives. Reeds have been bundled, and skins have been stretched to shape. At the turn of the 21st century, modern industrial and space-age materials such as plastics, composites, and exotic alloys have been added to the sculptor's ever-widening resources.

Although some prove more durable and resistant than others, all sculptural materials are susceptible to environmental agents that initiate deterioration, decay, and destruction. The approaches taken by the conservator to slow this deterioration are guided by a large number of complex considerations. The inherent nature of the material itself comes into play, as does the environment in which the sculpture has existed or will exist. The degree to which the sculpture has already deteriorated before conservation or restoration is also considered important. The original or intended purpose of the sculpture may have significant implications for its condition and for its survival, and various values (aesthetic, historic, cultural, religious, and monetary) may dramatically influence the conservator's course of action.

STONE SCULPTURE

With examples dating back to the enormous prehistoric statues of Easter Island, many types of stone have been employed over the centuries in sculpture. Some of these stones yield more readily to the sculptor's chisel (such as limestone, marble, and soapstone), while others, such as granite, are more difficult to carve but have proved more durable over time. All of these are susceptible to the deterioration caused by water. Water can either directly dissolve stone or wear it away by carrying abrasive particles over its surface. Water can also deteriorate stone when it freezes and turns to ice. Ice crystals have greater volume than liquid water, and when water is contained in the porous structure of stone and then freezes, the resulting ice crystals place enormous stress on the pore walls. This stress leads to microfractures in the structure of the stone. If the ice then melts, migrates to another location in the porous stone, and freezes again (as will happen with the changing of seasons in temperate climates), it begins what is called a "freeze-thaw cycle," in which repeated migration and freezing of the water cause the stone to lose cohesive strength, particularly near the surface. Freeze-thaw cycles can result in spalling, or delamination of the stone surface, eventually leaving no more than a shapeless mass in a relatively short amount of time.

Water can also carry soluble salts—such as the sodium chloride present in seawater or the nitrates found in groundwater polluted by fertilizers—into the porous structure of stone. These salts stay in solution and travel through the pores of the stone until the water begins to evaporate at the surface of the sculpture. Upon losing water, the salt will effloresce. Salt crystals, like ice crystals, have greater volume and place greater stresses on the pore walls, which leads to the same flaking or spalling caused by the freeze-thaw cycle. When the majority of the soluble salt crystallizes at the surface of the stone sculpture and forms a white powdery deposit, the process is defined as "surface-efflorescence." Although this process is unsightly and can cause damage, it is not as destructive as "subefflo-rescence," which occurs when the salt crystallizes in the pores of the stone below the actual surface. In the process of subefflorescence, the salt crystals are contained within the pores and hence place enormous pressure on the pore walls. Some types of stone contain large amounts of salt as part of their natural composition and as such are highly susceptible to damage under the right conditions. Other stones acquire salts from the environment, such as during burial, when they are exposed to groundwater laden with salt, or when they are exposed to water that has peculated through natural or man-made material (such as gypsum or cement) that also contains large amounts of salt.

Water also plays a role in the aggressive attack on stone by industrial air pollutants. Since the 19th century and to a limited degree well before that, the destructive properties of sulfur (released when fossil fuels are burned) have been well documented. Sulfur reacts in the atmosphere to form sulfur dioxide, which in turn combines with available moisture to form sulfuric acid. When in contact with marble or limestone (both of which are calcium carbonates), the sulfuric acid transforms the surface of the stone to gypsum (calcium sulfate). This transformation has several unfortunate results. First, the gypsum has greater volume and greater porosity, so it will hold more acidic water at the surface, continuing the acid attack on the underlying stone and encouraging other destructive processes such as biological activity (for example, the growth of mold). The gypsum crust formed often incorporates dark particulate matter from the polluted atmosphere, such as carbon, resulting in the unsightly black crusts seen on many urban buildings and monuments. This crust has a very different response to changes in temperature and will often crack or peel away, leaving fresh stone exposed to the same destructive cycle.

Biological deterioration of stone is also a concern. Root or vine growth can physically fracture marble, for example, if the root finds its way into a crack or fissure, similar to the way tree roots or weeds can fracture sidewalks or roads. Direct dissolution of stone by lichens and ivy is also possible, and the presence of such plants leads to the retention of water, which, as aforementioned, accelerates other destructive processes.

In the past, restoration of stone sculpture involved many aggressive methods aimed at erasing or disguising any damage or loss due to age, weathering, or accident. These techniques extended to the recutting of the sculpture or the reduction of the sculpted surface by means of abrasives or acids to remove damage or to "improve" the aesthetic appearance of the sculpture. Aesthetic dictates and fashion of the particular time in which the restoration was undertaken greatly influenced these choices, and often the sculpture became more of a product of the restorer's hand and time, rather than a work reflecting the intent of the original artist.

Today sculpture restoration (normally limited to the cleaning and repair of major damage) is guided by the various professional codes of ethics (such as the Code of Ethics and Guidelines for Practice of the American Institute for Conservation of Historic and Artistic Works [AIC]) followed by professional conservators. Original material and surface are carefully guarded, and the conservator takes great care not to alter the intent or "spirit" of the object or influence the way in which it may be interpreted. Missing areas are often left missing, and damage is often repaired only if doing so does not require unacceptably invasive treatments that are extensive in nature or that may not be reversible. Nonetheless, when replacing missing segments is acceptable or necessary, the conservator does this in such a manner as to make the replacements or additions apparent under close inspection or through using easily available inspection techniques.

Because soluble salts are so aggressively destructive to stone sculpture, their removal is of paramount importance if they are present in sufficient quantities. Traditionally, if the object is small enough to be submerged in water that is regularly refreshed, salts are soaked out until they are completely removed from the stone. However, when the sculpture is too large to submerge, too fragile to soak, or secured to a site, other methods must be employed. Also, some stones are composed of minerals that themselves will readily dissolve after prolonged contact with water; in such instances, poulticing is an optional method that avoids prolonged submersion of the stone in water and yet maximizes desalination. Poulticing involves wetting the sculpture with water and then placing a clay or paper pulp-based material mixed with water on the surface. As the water is drawn to the surface of the poultice by evaporation, the salts dissolved in the water are carried along and deposited in the poultice material. The poultice is then removed from the stone surface and the process repeated until all, or an acceptable amount, of the salts present are removed.

Stone can lose its cohesive strength when the material that binds the grains together becomes disrupted or lost through dissolution. In such a situation, the stone is described as "sugary," because the individual grains or crystals become easily dislodged and have the appearance of loose sugar granules. The stone may begin to delaminate in flakelike sections. In such cases, the cohesive and structural strength of the stone must be reinstated by the introduction of a consolidant. The characteristics of good stone consolidants include long-term stability and strength under adverse conditions (outdoors), the ability to penetrate deeply into the stone and provide even distribution of the final consolidating product throughout the stone, and a minimal effect upon the appearance of the stone once it is introduced (i.e., it should not change the colour or other characteristics such as translucency or opacity of the stone).

Consolidants can be divided into two major categories: mineral and synthetic consolidants. Among the mineral consolidants are "lime water," which is the introduction of a saturated water solution of calcium hydroxide into the matrix of a calcium-based stone (such as limestone or marble). Once the calcium hydroxide is deposited, its eventual interaction with atmospheric carbon dioxide forms a network of calcium carbonate, similar to that which makes up the stone itself. In a similar manner, the application of alkoxy silanes in recent decades offers the conservator a method by which amorphous silica can be introduced as a binder and strengthener for deteriorated sandstone. Some silanes will also impart water repellency to the stone. Synthetic polymer-based consolidants include acrylic polymers, epoxies, and polyesters. Although these are a considerable improvement over past materials such as wax and natural resins, some have proved unsuitable in certain environments and over long periods of exposure. Some epoxies have altered over a relatively short period of time and dramatically changed the appearance of the sculpture, while other synthetic consolidants have proved unable to penetrate deeply enough into the stone, and their application has resulted in a thin, dense, and impermeable crust that falls away owing to the buildup of salts or water vapour behind it.

A variety of coatings ranging from natural resins to waxes have been used for the protection of stone sculpture from either the outdoor elements or the deposition of dust and grime within the indoor environment. Acrylic polymers are now more commonly used for the less-demanding environments, whereas surface consolidants and water repellents based on silicone materials or hydrophobic silanes are often used for sculptures placed outdoors. Surface coatings can function to repel unwanted deposits or to serve as sacrificial layers that, when removed during regular maintenance, carry the deposits with them.

Cleaning was once undertaken with relatively aggressive methods such as abrasives, acids, and even chisels to remove the offending deposits or stains. More often than not, these approaches resulted in considerable damage to the original sculpted surface. At the turn of the 21st century, the professional conservator aggressively guards against any loss of original surface, even to the point of accepting the presence of a deposit or stain rather than endangering the original material of the sculpture. In some cases, the deposits that are obscuring the detail or subtle carving on the surface are in themselves informative and important and must be preserved rather than removed. In the case of many archaeological artifacts or ethnographic objects, for example, minute amounts of preserved material such as traces of pigment or deposits from original use can shed a great deal of light on the original appearance of the sculpture: its history, function, method of manufacture, and, to a degree, the artist's intent.

Contemporary techniques of cleaning may range from simple mechanical removal of the deposit with a common soft eraser to the use of surgical scalpels, often with the aid of a binocular microscope for more cautious and delicate cleaning. Small-scale power tools are commonly used when the deposit is extremely hard—for example, dental ultrasonic descalers can be used to remove hard calcite- or silica-based deposits or residues of modern cement and grout. The conservator sometimes employs microair abrasive equipment that uses fine particulate powders such as walnut shell or talc. The technique requires that the operator have considerable experience and skill so that the stone surface itself is not abraded. Chemical agents such as surfactants (agents that reduce surface tension between a liquid and a solid), chelates (agents that form compounds with metal ions, making them more easy to remove), or solvents can also be used either in local application using a small cotton swab or mixed in a poultice. Just as poulticing works as a means of desalination, it also can be used to eliminate deposits and stains. Poulticing material may include clays (such as sepiolite, a magnesium trisilicate clay), paper pulp, or gel materials such as carboxymethylcellulose. Steam cleaning and water misting (sometimes called "nebulization") are also often employed in the cleaning process, though like all the techniques already mentioned, they must be cautiously applied to ensure that only the desired deposit or grime is removed, without damaging the stone surface or other decorative elements.

First used in the 1970s to clean the black pollution crusts from stone architectural sculpture, laser technology has rapidly developed as a promising method for cleaning stone surfaces. Laser energy dislodges or vaporizes the offending material that is normally of a darker colour than the stone. The laser has become one of the most promising tools for future use in conservation due to the advancement of more commonly available units, a relative drop in cost of the equipment, and a greater familiarity with laser technology in the field of conservation.

METAL SCULPTURE

Metal sculpture ranges from solid-cast statuettes of the ancient Near East to the massive steel public monuments of the late 20th century. In most instances, the deterioration of metal sculpture is due to the reversion of the metal to a more stable mineral state. In the case of iron, the process is most commonly known as "rusting" and results in a red-brown, powdery mineral iron oxide. Copper and its alloys most commonly alter to the green or blue carbonates of copper, malachite, or azurite or to the red-oxide mineral cuprite. Copper and its alloys may also quickly corrode in the presence of chloride by the cyclic process called "bronze disease," during which copper is altered to copper chloride, a powdery white-blue product. Silver tarnishes rapidly even in the presence of minute amounts of sulfur, and lead will quickly corrode in the presence of acetic acid. Common to all of the processes is the presence of water, which is needed to initiate and complete the corrosion of the base metal to a more voluminous and less cohesive mineral product.

In the past, the treatment of metal sculptures often involved completely stripping the surface until it was free of all corrosion product or alteration. Abrasive techniques such as sandblasting or microbead blasting were regularly used, as was chemical stripping (which dissolved the mineral alteration products) and electro-chemical reduction, which also stripped the surface of any corrosion products and of "patina," the term usually given to corrosion products that are either naturally occurring or artificially formed on the metal surface. Patinas are valued for aesthetic beauty and for the authenticity that they lend the object. Today treatment of metal sculptures is far more conservative than in the past. Although sculpture may be polished (as in the case of silver sculpture that has been tarnished) or stripped of its alteration patina (as in the case of some monumental outdoor sculptures), alteration products are carefully evaluated for their importance and authenticity before their removal is considered, and patinas are far more often protected than removed. Any treatment that results in the reshaping of the metal or in any irreversible addition, such as soldering or welding to secure broken segments, is now considered with great caution.

At the turn of the 21st century, the conservator's main intervention in the process of corrosion involved providing a more benign environment (usually meaning as dry as possible and as free of harmful pollutants as possible) and maintaining the sculpture's stability through a series of preventive maintenance procedures, such as regular cleaning and the application of protective coatings. Regular maintenance has proved to be highly cost-effective and successful in the preservation of outdoor sculpture over the long term. Regular cleaning and coating (with waxes or synthetic polymers or both, which sometimes contain corrosion inhibitors) have kept corrosion processes in check, even in aggressive and polluted urban environments. In some cases, however, the conservator's only option is to recommend

The bronze equestrian statue of General William Tecumseh Sherman with a figure of Victory by sculptor Augustus Saint-Gaudens was restored and later re-gilded. It is located in New York City and was dedicated in 1903.

that the sculptures be removed from the outdoor environment, placed in a protected area, and replaced by a replica made of a more-resistant material.

Although cleaning of metal sculpture can include the total removal of all corrosion products, including those termed and valued as patina, a more conservative approach continues to develop within the field, which recognizes the value of naturally occurring change to the metal surface. In the case of archaeological material and ethnographic sculpture, the corrosion products may hold remnants of original surface treatments or remains of associated materials or evidence of use. This evidence must be carefully studied, and a full understanding of the sculpture's importance (now and in the future) must be weighed against its loss by cleaning.

WOOD SCULPTURE

Although relatively little wood sculpture survives from prehistorical and early historical periods, an enormous amount of sculpture was produced in the last millennium, particularly the polychrome sculptures of western European religious devotion and those of India, China, Japan, and other Asian nations. Wood is a very open and porous structure, the bulk of which is water, absorbed or chemically bound to its thin-walled structural cells. Like many plant materials, wood responds to changes in the humidity of its surrounding environment, taking up available water to reach equilibrium with the environment or, conversely, giving up water if the surrounding air is dryer. Dimensional changes to the wood occur when this exchange takes place. As wood takes up water, it will swell. As it loses water, it will shrink, sometimes dramatically. Both actions induce considerable stresses on the structure of the wood, resulting in irreversible warping or complete splitting of the wood section. Additionally, the physical strain placed on the structure by continual expansion and contraction weakens the wood or may cause further serious damage to wood already weakened by insect attack or age. When decorated with paint, wood will respond to heat and moisture with greater movement, destroying the bond between the wood and the less elastic paint and ground preparation, resulting in the painted decoration's flaking away from the surface.

Wood can also be a food source or a nesting place for a variety of insects such as wood-boring beetles, termites, and grubs. Infestation can be so severe that the sculpture loses all of its structural strength and collapses. Wood can also be damaged by a variety of fungi and bacteria with similar results.

The predominant concern regarding the preservation of wood is the control of the environment. Exposure to light, particularly the ultraviolet and shorter wavelengths of the visible spectrum, results in both the chemical and physical alteration of all organic material, including wood. Wood can become darker or lighter or lose its structural integrity through the action of light energy acting as a catalyst for other chemical reactions.

Appropriate and stable temperature and humidity levels and an environment low in ultraviolet radiation, illumination, and pollutants can ensure the slowing of any deterioration. Regular dusting and general maintenance of the sculpture, as well as vigilant actions to keep damaging insects away, are also paramount. When intervention is necessary with wood sculpture, it normally involves some form of consolidation, either of the wood sculpture's structure or of its decorative surface. The range of consolidants for each of these actions is broad, including synthetic acrylic polymers, organic-based natural resins, and animal glues.

CHAPTER THREE

METHODS AND TECHNIQUES

Although a sculptor may specialize in, say, stone carving or direct metalwork, the art of sculpture is not identifiable with any particular craft or set of crafts. It presses into its service whatever crafts suit its purposes. Technologies developed for more utilitarian purposes are often easily adapted for sculpture; in fact, useful artifacts and sculptured images have often been produced in the same workshop, sometimes by the same craftsman. The methods and techniques employed in producing a pot, a bronze harness trapping, a decorative stone molding or column, a carved wooden newel post, or even a fibreglass car body are essentially the same as those used in sculpture. For example, the techniques of repoussé, metal casting, blacksmithing, sheet-metal work, and welding, which are used for the production of functional artifacts and decorative metalwork, are also used in metal sculpture, and the preparation, forming, glazing, decoration, and firing of clay are basically the same in both utilitarian pottery and pottery sculpture. The new techniques used by sculptors today are closely related to new techniques applied in building and industrial manufacture.

REPOUSSÉ

Repoussé is a method of decorating metals in which parts of the design are raised in relief from the back or the inside of the article by means of hammers and punches; definition and detail can then be added from the front by chasing or engraving. The name repoussé is derived from the French *pousser*, "to push forward." This ancient technique, which has been used extensively throughout the history of metalworking, achieved widespread popularity in Europe during the 16th, 17th, and 18th centuries.

THE SCULPTOR AS DESIGNER AND AS CRAFTSMAN

The conception of an artifact or a work of art—its form, imaginative content, and expressiveness—is the concern of a designer, and it should be distinguished from the execution of the work in a particular technique and material, which is the task of a craftsman. A sculptor often functions as both designer and craftsman, but these two aspects of sculpture may be separated.

Certain types of sculpture depend considerably for their aesthetic effect on the way in which their material has been directly manipulated by the artist

American sculptor Frank Gallo (b. 1933) works on a clay model in his studio. He often worked in epoxy resin but today mostly uses cast paper, a process he developed.

himself. The direct, expressive handling of clay in a model by Rodin or the use of the chisel in the stiacciato (very low) reliefs of the 15th-century Florentine sculptor Donatello could no more have been delegated to a craftsman than could the brushwork of Rembrandt. The actual physical process of working materials is for many sculptors an integral part of the art of sculpture, and their response to the working qualities of the material—such as its plasticity, hardness, and texture—is evident in the finished work. Design and craftsmanship are intimately fused in such a work, which is a highly personal expression.

Even when the direct handling of material is not as vital as this to the expressiveness of the work, it still may be impossible to separate the roles of the artist as designer and craftsman. The qualities and interrelationships of forms may be so subtle and complex that they cannot be adequately specified and communicated to a craftsman. Moreover, many aspects of the design may actually be contributed during the process of working. Michelangelo's way of working, for example, enabled him to change his mind about important aspects of composition as the work proceeded.

A complete fusion of design and craftsmanship may not be possible if a project is a large one or if the sculptor is too old or too weak to do all of the work himself. The sheer physical labour of making a large sculpture can be considerable, and sculptors from Phidias in the 5th century BCE to Henry Moore in the 20th century, for example, have employed pupils and assistants to help with it. Usually the sculptor delegates the time-consuming first stages of the work or some of its less important parts to his assistants and executes the final stages or the most important parts himself.

On occasion, a sculptor may function like an architect or industrial designer. He may do no direct work at all on the finished sculpture, his contribution being to supply exhaustive specifications in the form of drawings and perhaps scale models for a work that is to be entirely fabricated by craftsmen. Obviously, such a procedure excludes the possibility of direct, personal expression through the handling of the materials; thus, works of this kind usually have the same anonymous, impersonal quality as architecture and industrial design. An impersonal approach to sculpture was favoured by many sculptors of the 1960s such as William Tucker,

Donald Judd, and William Turnbull. They used the skilled anonymous workmanship of industrial fabrications to make their large-scale, extremely precise, simple sculptural forms that are called "primary structures."

GENERAL METHODS

Broadly speaking, the stages in the production of a major work of sculpture conform to the following pattern: the commission; the preparation, submission, and acceptance of the design; the selection and preparation of materials; the forming of materials; surface finishing; installation or presentation.

Almost all of the sculpture of the past and some present-day sculpture originate in a demand made upon the sculptor from outside, usually in the form of a direct commission or through a competition. If the commission is for a portrait or a private sculpture, the client may only require to see examples of the artist's previous work, but if it is a public commission, the sculptor is usually expected to submit drawings and maquettes (small-scale, three-dimensional sketch models) that give an idea of the nature of the finished work and its relation to the site.

He may be free to choose his own subject matter or theme, or it may be more or less strictly prescribed. A medieval master sculptor, for example, received the program for a complex scheme of church sculpture from theological advisers, and Renaissance contracts for sculpture were often extremely specified and detailed. Today a great deal of sculpture is not commissioned. It arises out of the sculptor's private concern with form and imagery, and he works primarily to satisfy himself.

When the work is finished he may exhibit and attempt to sell it in an art gallery.

Most of the materials used by 20th-century sculptors were readily available in a usable form from builders' or sculptors' suppliers, but certain kinds of sculpture may involve a good deal of preparatory work on the materials. A sculptor may visit a stone quarry in order to select the material for a large project and to have it cut into blocks of the right size and shape. And since stone is costly to transport and best carved when freshly quarried, he may decide to do all of his work at the quarry. Because stone is extremely heavy, the sculptor must have the special equipment required for maneuvering even small blocks into position for carving. A wood-carver requires a supply of well-seasoned timber and may keep a quantity of logs and blocks in store. A modeler needs a good supply of clay of the right kind. For large terra-cottas he may require a specially made-up clay body, or he may work at a brickworks, using the local clay and firing in the brick kilns.

The main part of the sculptor's work, the shaping of the material itself by modeling, carving, or constructional techniques, may be a long and arduous process, perhaps extending over a number of years and requiring assistants. Much of the work, especially architectural decoration, may be carried out at the site, or in situ.

To improve its weathering qualities, to bring out the characteristics of its material to the best advantage, or to make it more decorative or realistic, sculpture is usually given a special surface finish. It may be rubbed down and polished, patinated, metal plated, gilded, painted, inlaid with other materials, and so on.

Finally, the installation of sculpture may be a complex and important part of the work. The positioning and fixing of large architectural sculpture may involve cooperation with builders and engineers; fountains may involve elaborate plumbing; and the design and placing of outdoor bases, or plinths, in relation to the site and the spectator may require careful thought. The choice of the materials, shape, and proportions of the base even for a small work requires a considerable amount of care.

CARVING

Whatever material is used, the essential features of the direct method of carving are the same; the sculptor starts with a solid mass of material and reduces it systematically to the desired form. After he has blocked out the main masses and planes that define the outer limits of the forms, he works progressively over the whole sculpture, first carving the larger containing forms and planes and then the smaller ones until eventually the surface details are reached. Then he gives the surface whatever finish is required. Even with a preliminary model as a guide, the sculptor's concept

The unfinished sculpture of St. Matthew by Michelangelo gives the viewer the feeling that the figure wants to break away from the marble block.

constantly evolves and clarifies as the work proceeds; thus, as he adapts his design to the nature of the carving process and the material, his work develops as an organic whole.

The process of direct carving imposes a characteristic order on the forms of sculpture. The faces of the original block, slab, or cylinder of material can usually still be sensed, existing around the finished work as a kind of implied spatial envelope limiting the extension of the forms in space and connecting their highest points across space. In a similar way, throughout the whole carving, smaller forms and planes can be seen as contained within implied larger ones. Thus, an ordered sequence of containing forms and planes, from the largest to the smallest, gives unity to the work.

INDIRECT CARVING

All of the great sculptural traditions of the past used the direct method of carving, but in Western civilization during the 19th and early 20th centuries it became customary for stone and, to a lesser extent, wood sculpture to be produced by the indirect method. This required the production of a finished clay model that was subsequently cast in plaster and then reproduced in stone or wood in a more or less mechanical way by means of a pointing machine. Usually the carving was not done by the sculptor himself. At its worst, this procedure results in a carved copy of a design that was conceived in terms of clay modeling. Although indirect carving does not achieve aesthetic qualities that are typical of carved sculpture, it does not necessarily result in bad sculpture. Rodin's marble sculptures, for example, are generally considered great works of art even by those who object to the indirect methods by which they were produced. The indirect method has been steadily losing ground since the revival of direct carving in the early 20th century, and today it is in general disrepute among carvers.

CARVING TOOLS AND TECHNIQUES

The tools used for carving differ with the material to be carved. Stone is carved mostly with steel tools that resemble cold chisels. To knock off the corners and angles of a block, a tool called a pitcher is driven into the surface with a heavy iron hammer. The pitcher is a thick, chisel-like tool with a wide beveled edge that breaks rather than cuts the stone. The heavy point then does the main roughing out, followed by the fine point, which may be used to within a short distance of the final surface. These pointed tools are hammered into the surface at an angle that causes the stone to break off in chips of varying sizes. Claw chisels, which have toothed edges, may then be worked in all directions over the surface, removing the stone in granule form and thus refining the surface forms. Flat chisels are used for finishing the surface carving and for cutting sharp detail. There are many other special tools, including stone gouges, drills, toothed hammers (known as bushhammers or bouchardes), and, often used today, power-driven pneumatic tools, for pounding away the surface of the stone. The surface can be polished with a variety of processes and materials.

Because medieval carvers worked mostly in softer stones and made great use of flat chisels, their work tends to have an edgy, cut quality and to be freely and deeply carved. In contrast is the work done in hard stones by people who lacked metal tools hard enough to cut the stone. Egyptian granite sculpture, for

Wood-carving tools include gauges, chisels, rasps, files, mallets, saws, and drills. Sandpaper is used to give pieces a smooth finish.

example, was produced mainly by abrasion, that is, by pounding the surface and rubbing it down with abrasive materials. The result is a compact sculpture, not deeply hollowed out, with softened edges and flowing surfaces. It usually has a high degree of tactile appeal.

Although the process of carving is fundamentally the same for wood or stone, the physical structure of wood demands tools of a different type. For the first blocking out of a wood carving a sculptor may use saws and axes, but his principal tools are a wide range of wood-carver's gouges. The sharp, curved edge of a gouge cuts easily through the bundles of fibre and when used properly will not split the wood. Flat chisels are also used, especially for carving sharp details. Wood rasps, or coarse files, and sandpaper can be used to give the surface a smooth finish, or, if preferred, it can be left with a faceted, chiseled appearance. Wood-carving tools have hardwood handles and are struck with round, wooden mallets. African wood sculptors use a variety of adzes rather than gouges and mallets. Ivory

A FILE

In hardware and metalworking, a file is a tool of hardened steel in the form of a bar or rod with many small cutting edges raised on its longitudinal surfaces; it is used for smoothing

(CONTINUED ON THE NEXT PAGE)

(CONTINUED FROM THE PREVIOUS PAGE)

or forming objects, especially of metal. The cutting or abrading action of the file results from rubbing it, usually by hand, against the workpiece.

Files are classified according to their cross-sectional shapes, the form of the cutting edges, and the coarseness of the cut (i.e., the number of teeth per inch or centimetre). There are at least 20 different cross-sectional shapes; the most common are rectangular with various width-to-thickness ratios, square, triangular, round or rattail, and half round. There are three general classifications of tooth form: single-cut, double-cut, and rasp. The single-cut file has rows of parallel teeth cut diagonally across the working surfaces. The double-cut file has rows of teeth crossing each other. Rasp teeth are disconnected and round on top; they are formed by raising small pieces of material from the surface of the file with a punch. Rasp files, or rasps, are usually very coarse and are used primarily on wood and soft materials.

Classification according to coarseness or spacing of the teeth is confined to single- and double-cut files. There are six main classes: rough, coarse, bastard, second-cut, smooth, and dead smooth. The number of teeth per inch varies considerably for different shapes and sizes.

is carved with an assortment of saws, knives, rasps, files, chisels, drills, and scrapers.

MODELING

In contrast to the reductive process of carving, modeling is essentially a building-up process in which the sculpture grows organically from the inside. Numerous plastic materials are used for modeling. The main ones are clay, plaster, and wax, but concrete, synthetic resins, plastic wood, stucco, and even molten metal can also be modeled. A design modeled in plastic materials may be intended for reproduction by casting in more permanent and rigid materials, such as metal, plaster, concrete, and fibreglass, or it may itself be made rigid and more permanent through the self-setting properties of its materials (for example, plaster) or by firing.

Clay and wax are the most common modeling materials, and the artist's hands are the main tools, though metal and wood implements are often employed in shaping. Modeling is an ancient technique, as indicated by prehistoric clay figurines from Egypt and the Middle East.

Unlike carving, corrections are possible during modeling, and the result—fired clay or preserved wax—is not as permanent as a stone or wood carving. Modeled work, however, may be reproduced in stone by pointing (transferring the proportions of the model to the block of stone by mechanical means) or, in metal, by casting. Finished works modeled in clay or wax should not be confused with *bozzetti*, small wax or clay models serving as preliminary sketches for large carvings, or maquettes,

AN ARMATURE

In sculpture, an armature is a skeleton or framework used by an artist to support a figure being modeled in soft plastic material. An armature can be made from any material that is damp-resistant and rigid enough to hold such plastic materials as moist clay and plaster, which are applied to and shaped around it. Pieces of thick wire, a few blocks of wood nailed together, or a galvanized iron pipe secured to a baseboard can serve as the armature for a life-sized head or a small standing figure. Larger pieces of sculpture are supported by more complicated armatures constructed of lead pipe, iron rods, or pipes and wood. A combination of these materials is used in the huge armatures required for monumental sculpture. Armatures for large models were used as early as the Renaissance.

small, relatively finished models used to present proposals for monumental projects.

MODELING FOR CASTING

The material most widely used for making positive models for casting is clay. A small, compact design or a low relief can be modeled solidly in clay without any internal support,

but a large clay model must be formed over a strong armature made of wood and metal. Since the armature may
be very elaborate and can only be altered slightly, if at all,
once work has started, the modeler must have a fairly clear
idea from his drawings and maquettes of the arrangement
of the main shapes of the finished model. The underlying
main masses of the sculpture are built up firmly over the
armature, and then the smaller forms, surface modeling,
and details are modeled over them. The modeler's chief
tools are his fingers, but for fine work he may use a variety
of wooden modeling tools to apply the clay and wire loop
tools to cut it away. Reliefs are modeled on a vertical or
nearly vertical board. The clay is keyed, or secured, onto
the board with galvanized nails or wood laths. The amount
of armature required depends on the height of the relief
and the weight of clay involved.

To make a cast in metal, a foundry requires from the
sculptor a model made of a rigid material, usually plaster. The sculptor can produce this either by modeling in
clay and then casting in plaster from the clay model or by
modeling directly in plaster. For direct plaster modeling, a
strong armature is required because the material is brittle.
The main forms may be built up roughly over the armature in expanded wire and then covered in plaster-soaked
scrim (a loosely woven sacking). This provides a hollow
base for the final modeling, which is done by applying plaster with metal spatulas and by scraping and cutting down
with rasps and chisels.

Fibreglass and concrete sculptures are cast in plaster
molds taken from the sculptor's original model. The model
is usually clay rather than plaster because if the forms of
the sculpture are at all complex it is easier to remove a
plaster mold from a soft clay model than from a model in a
rigid material, such as plaster.

A great deal of the metal sculpture of the past, including Nigerian, Indian, and many Renaissance bronzes, was produced by the direct lost-wax process, which involves a special modeling technique. The design is first modeled in some refractory material to within a fraction of an inch of the final surface, and then the final modeling is done in a layer of wax, using the fingers and also metal tools, which can be heated to make the wax more pliable. Medallions are often produced from wax originals, but because of their small size they can be solid-cast and therefore do not require a core.

MODELING FOR POTTERY SCULPTURE

To withstand the stresses of firing, a large pottery sculpture must be hollow and of an even thickness. There are two main ways of achieving this. In the process of hollow modeling, which is typical of the potter's approach to form, the main forms of the clay model are built up directly as hollow forms with walls of a roughly even thickness. The methods of building are similar to those employed for making hand-built pottery—coiling, pinching, and slabbing. The smaller forms and details are then added, and the finished work is allowed to dry out slowly and thoroughly before firing. The process of solid modeling is more typical of the sculptor's traditional approach to form. The sculpture is modeled in solid clay, sometimes over a carefully considered armature, by the sculptor's usual methods of clay modeling. Then it is cut open and hollowed out, and the armature, if there is one, is removed. The pieces are then rejoined and the work is dried out and fired.

GENERAL CHARACTERISTICS
OF MODELED SCULPTURE

The process of modeling affects the design of sculpture in three important ways. First, the forms of the sculpture tend to be ordered from the inside. There are no external containing forms and planes, as in carved sculpture. The overall design of the work—its main volumes, proportions, and axial arrangement—is determined by the underlying forms, and the smaller forms, surface modeling, and decorative details are all formed around and sustained by this underlying structure. Second, because its extension into space is not limited by the dimensions of a block of material, modeled sculpture tends to be much freer and more expansive in its spatial design than carved sculpture. If the tensile strength of metal is to be exploited in the finished work, there is almost unlimited freedom; designs for brittle materials such as concrete or plaster are more limited. Third, the plasticity of clay and wax encourages a fluent, immediate kind of manipulation, and many sculptors, such as Auguste Rodin, Giacomo Manzù, and Sir Jacob Epstein, like to preserve this record of their direct handling of the medium in their finished work. Their approach contrasts with that of the Benin and Indian bronze sculptors, who refined the surfaces of their work to remove all traces of personal "handwriting."

CONSTRUCTING AND ASSEMBLING

A constructed or assembled sculpture is made by joining preformed pieces of material. It differs radically in principle from carved and modeled sculpture, both of which are fabricated out of a homogeneous mass of material. Constructed sculpture is made out of such basic preformed components as metal tubes, rods, plates, bars, and sheets; wooden laths, planks, dowels, and blocks; laminated timbers and chipboards; sheets of Perspex, Formica, and glass; fabrics; and wires and threads. These are cut to various sizes and may be either shaped before they are assembled or used as they are. The term *assemblage* is usually reserved for constructed sculpture that incorporates any of a vast array of ready-made, so-called found objects, such as old boilers, typewriters, engine components, mirrors, chairs, and table legs and other bits of old furniture.

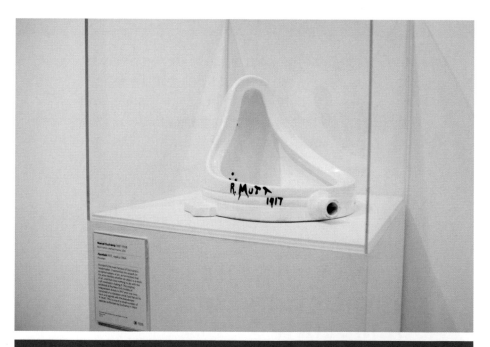

Marcel Duchamp's *Fountain*, a porcelain urinal, is a ready-made, an everyday object designated as art. This is a 1964 replica of the 1917 original, which is now lost.

Numerous techniques are employed for joining these components, most of them derived from crafts other than traditional sculptural ones, for example: metal welding and brazing, wood joinery, bolting, screwing, riveting, nailing, and bonding with new powerful adhesives.

The use of constructional techniques to produce sculpture is the main technical development of the art in recent years. Among the reasons for its popularity are that it lends itself readily to an emphasis on the spatial aspects of sculpture that preoccupied so many 20th-century artists; it is quicker than carving and modeling; it is considered by many sculptors and critics to be especially appropriate to a technological civilization; and it is opening up new fields of imagery and new types of symbolism and form.

For constructed "gallery" sculpture, almost any materials and techniques are likely to be used, and the products are often extremely ephemeral. But architectural sculpture, outdoor sculpture, and indeed any sculpture that is actually used must be constructed in a safe and at least reasonably permanent manner. The materials and techniques employed are therefore somewhat restricted. Metal sculpture constructed by riveting, bolting, and, above all, welding and brazing is best for outdoor use.

DIRECT METAL SCULPTURE

The introduction of the oxyacetylene welding torch as a sculptor's tool has revolutionized metal sculpture in recent years. A combination of welding and forging techniques was pioneered by the Spanish sculptor Julio González around 1930, and during the 1940s and 1950s it became a major sculptural technique, particularly in Britain and in the United States, where its greatest exponent was David Smith. In the 1960s and early 1970s, more sophisticated electric welding processes were replacing flame welding.

Welding equipment can be used for joining and cutting metal. A welded joint is made by melting and fusing together the surfaces of two pieces of metal, usually with the addition of a small quantity of the same metal as a filler. The metal most widely used for welded sculpture is mild steel, but other metals can be welded. In a brazed joint, the parent metals are not actually fused together but are joined by an alloy that melts at a lower temperature than the parent metals. Brazing is particularly useful for making joints between different kinds of metal, which cannot be done by welding, and for joining nonferrous metals. Forging is the direct shaping of metal by bending, hammering, and cutting.

Direct metalworking techniques have opened up whole new ranges of form to the sculptor—open skeletal structures, linear and highly extended forms, and complex, curved sheet forms. Constructed metal sculpture may be precise and clean, as that of Minimalist sculptors Donald Judd and Phillip King, or it may exploit the textural effects of molten metal in a free, "romantic" manner.

REPRODUCTION AND SURFACE-FINISHING TECHNIQUES

Casting and molding processes are used in sculpture either for making copies of existing sculpture or as

THE LOST-WAX PROCESS

The lost-wax process, also called cire-perdue, is a method of metal casting in which a molten metal is poured into a mold that has been created by means of a wax model. Once the mold is made, the wax model is melted and drained away. A hollow core can be effected by the introduction of a heat-proof core that prevents the molten metal from totally filling the mold. Common on every continent except Australia, the lost-wax method dates from the 3rd millennium BCE and has sustained few changes since then.

To cast a clay model in bronze, a mold is made from the model, and the inside of this negative mold is brushed with melted wax to the desired thickness of the final bronze. After removal of the mold, the resultant wax shell is filled with a heat-resistant mixture. Wax tubes, which provide ducts for pouring bronze during casting and vents for the noxious gases produced in the process, are fitted to the outside of the wax shell, which may be modeled or adjusted by the artist. Metal pins are hammered through the shell into the core to secure it. Next, the prepared wax shell is

(CONTINUED ON THE NEXT PAGE)

(CONTINUED FROM THE PREVIOUS PAGE)

completely covered in layers of heat-resistant plaster, and the whole is inverted and placed in an oven. During heating, the plaster dries and the wax runs out through the ducts created by the wax tubes. The plaster mold is then packed in sand, and molten bronze is poured through the ducts, filling the space left by the wax. When cool, the outer plaster and core are removed, and the bronze may receive finishing touches.

essential stages in the production of a finished work. Many materials are used for making molds and casts, and some of the methods are complex and highly skilled. Only a broad outline of the main methods can be given here.

CASTING AND MOLDING

These are used for producing a single cast from a soft, plastic original, usually clay. They are especially useful for producing master casts for subsequent reproduction in metal. The basic procedure is as follows. First, the mold is built up in liquid plaster over the original clay model; for casting reliefs, a one-piece mold may be sufficient, but for sculpture in the round a mold in at least two sections is required. Second, when the plaster is set, the mold is divided and removed from the clay model. Third, the mold is cleaned, reassembled, and filled with a self-setting material such as plaster, concrete, or fibreglass-reinforced resin. Fourth, the mold is carefully chipped away from the cast. This involves the destruction of the mold—hence the term "waste" mold. The order of reassembling and filling the mold may be reversed; fibreglass and resin, for example, are "laid up" in the mold pieces before they are reassembled.

Plaster piece molds are used for producing more than one cast from a soft or rigid original and are especially good for reproducing existing sculpture and for slip casting. Before the invention of flexible molds, piece molds were used for producing wax casts for metal casting by the lost-wax process. A piece mold is built up in sections that can be withdrawn from the original model without damaging it. The number of sections depends on the complexity of the form and on the amount of undercutting; tens, or even hundreds, of pieces may be required for really large, complex works. The mold sections are carefully keyed together and supported by a plaster case. When the mold has been filled, it can be removed section by section from the cast and used again. Piece molding is a highly skilled and laborious process.

Made of such materials as gelatin, vinyl, and rubber, flexible molds are used for producing more than one cast; they offer a much simpler alternative to piece molding when the original model is a rigid one with complex forms and undercuts. The material is melted and poured around the original positive in sections, if necessary. Being flexible, the mold easily pulls away from a rigid surface without causing damage. While it is being filled (with wax, plaster, concrete, and fibreglass-reinforced resins), the mold must be surrounded by a plaster case to prevent distortion.

The lost-wax process is the traditional method of casting metal sculpture. It requires a positive, which consists of a core made of a refractory material and an outer layer of wax. The positive can be produced either by direct modeling in wax over a prepared core, in which case the process is known as direct lost-wax casting, or by casting in a piece mold or flexible mold taken from a master cast. The wax positive is invested with a mold made of refractory materials and is then heated to a temperature that will drive off all mois-ture and melt out all the wax, leaving a narrow cavity between the core and the investment. Molten metal is then poured into this cavity. When the metal has cooled down and solidified, the investment is broken away, and the core is removed from inside the cast. The process is, of course, much more complex than this simple outline suggests. Care has to be taken to suspend the core within the mold by means of metal pins, and a structure of channels must be made in the mold that will enable the metal to reach all parts of the cavity and permit the mold gases to escape. A considerable amount of filing and chasing of the cast is usually required after casting is completed.

While the lost-wax process is used for producing complex, refined metal castings, sand molding is more suitable for simpler types of form and for sculpture in which a certain roughness of surface does not matter. Recent improvements in the quality of sand castings and the invention of the "lost-pattern" process have resulted in a much wider use of sand casting as a means of produc-ing sculpture. A sand mold, made of special sand held together by a binder, is built up around a rigid positive, usu-ally in a number of sections held together in metal boxes. For a hollow casting, a core is required that will fit inside the negative mold, leaving a narrow cavity as in the lost-wax process. The molten metal is poured into this cavity.

The lost-pattern process is used for the production by sand molding of single casts in metal. After a positive made of expanded polystyrene is firmly embedded in casting sand, molten metal is poured into the mold straight onto the expanded foam original. The heat of the metal causes the foam to pass off into vapour and disappear, leaving a negative mold to be filled by the metal. Channels for the metal to run in and for the gases to escape are made in the mold, as in the lost-wax process. The method is used mainly for producing solid castings in aluminum that can be welded or riveted together to make the finished sculpture.

Slip casting is primarily a potter's technique that can be used for repetition casting of small pottery sculptures. Liquid clay, or slip, is poured into a plaster piece mold. Some of the water in the slip is absorbed by the plaster and a layer of stiffened clay collects on the surface of the mold. When this layer is thick enough to form a cast, the excess slip is poured off and the mold is removed. The hollow clay cast is then dried and fired.

Simple casts for pottery sculpture, mainly tiles and low reliefs, can be prepared by pressing clay into a rigid mold. More complex forms can be built up from a number of separately press-cast pieces. Simple terra-cotta molds can be made by pressing clay around a rigid positive form. After firing, these press molds can be used for press casting.

POINTING

A sculpture can be reproduced by transposing measurements taken all over its surface to a copy. The process is made accurate and thorough by the use of a pointing machine, which is an arrangement of adjustable metal arms and pointers that are set to the position of any point on the surface of a three-dimensional form and then used to locate the corresponding point on the surface of a copy. If the copy is a stone one, the block is drilled to the depth measured by the pointing machine. When a number of points have been fixed by drilling, the stone is cut away to the required depth. For accurate pointing, a vast number of points have to be taken, and the final surface is approached gradually. The main use of pointing has been for the indirect method of carving.

Enlarged and reduced copies of sculpture can also be produced with the aid of mechanical devices. A sophisticated reducing machine that works on the principle of the pantograph (an instrument for copying on any predetermined scale, consisting of four light, rigid bars jointed in parallelogram form) is used in minting for scaling down the sculptor's original model to coin size.

SURFACE FINISHING

Surface finishes for sculpture can be either natural—bringing the material of the sculpture itself to a finish—or applied. Almost all applied surface finishes preserve as well as decorate.

SMOOTHING AND POLISHING

Many sculptural materials have a natural beauty of colour and texture that can be brought out by smoothing and polishing. Stone carvings are smoothed by rubbing down with a graded series of coarse and fine abrasives, such as carborundum, sandstone, emery, pumice, and whiting, all used while the stone is wet. Some stones, such as marble and granite, will take a high gloss; others are too coarse-grained to be polished and can only be smoothed to a granular finish. Wax is sometimes used to give stone a final polish.

The natural beauty of wood is brought out by sandpapering or scraping and then waxing or oiling. Beeswax and linseed oil are the traditional materials, but a wide range of waxes and oils is currently available.

Ivory is polished with gentle abrasives such as pumice and whiting, applied with a damp cloth.

Concrete can be rubbed down, like stone, with water and abrasives, which both smooth the surface and expose the aggregate. Some concretes can be polished.

Metals are rubbed down manually with steel wool and emery paper and polished with various metal polishes. A high-gloss polish can be given to metals by means of power-driven buffing wheels used in conjunction with abrasives and polishes. Clear lacquers are applied to preserve the polish.

PAINTING

Stone, wood, terra-cotta, metal, fibreglass, and plaster can all be painted in a reasonably durable manner provided that the surfaces are properly prepared and suitable primings and paints are used. In the past, stone and wood carvings were often finished with a coating of gesso (plaster of paris or gypsum prepared with glue) that served both as a final modeling material for delicate surface detail and as a priming for painting. Historically, the painting and gilding of sculpture were usually left to specialists. In Greek relief sculpture, actual details of the composition were often omitted at the carving stage and left for the painter to insert. In the 15th century, the great Flemish painter Rogier van der Weyden undertook the painting of sculpture as part of his work.

Modern paint technology has made an enormous range of materials available. Constructed sculptures are often finished with mechanical grinders and sanders and then sprayed with high-quality cellulose paints.

GILDING

The surfaces of wood, stone, and plaster sculpture can be decorated with gold, silver, and other metals that are applied in leaf or powder form over a suitable priming. Metals, especially bronze, were often fire-gilded, that is, treated with an amalgam of gold and mercury that was

Lorenzo Ghiberti's gilded bronze relief panels from the *Gates of Paradise* (1425–52) were restored and are in the Museo dell'Opera del Duomo in Florence. Replicas adorn the entrance to the Baptistery of San Giovanni.

ABOUT GILDING

The ancient Egyptians were master gilders, as evidenced by the overlays of thin gold leaf on their royal mummy cases and furniture. From early times the Chinese ornamented wood, pottery, and textiles with beautiful designs in gold. The Greeks not only gilded wood, masonry, and marble sculpture but also fire-gilded metal by applying a gold amalgam to it and driving off the mercury with heat, leaving a coating of gold on the metal surface. From the Greeks, the Romans acquired the art that made their temples and palaces resplendent with brilliant gilding.

Certain basic procedures are pertinent to all types of gilding. For example, the ground to be gilded must be carefully prepared by priming. Flat paints, lacquers, or sealing glues are used, according to the nature of the ground material. Metals subject to corrosion may be primed and protected by red lead or iron oxide paints. After the ground has been prepared and is thoroughly dry, the gilder lays out his design on the ground with pencil or chalk. To create an adhesive surface, the area to be gilded is sized. The type of size used depends on the kind of surface to be gilded

(CONTINUED ON THE NEXT PAGE)

(CONTINUED FROM THE PREVIOUS PAGE)

and on whether it is desirable for the size to dry quickly or slowly. When the size has dried enough so that it just adheres to the fingertips, it is ready to receive or retain the gold leaf or powder.

Beating gold into leaves as thin as 1/280,000 inch (0.00009 millimetre) is done largely by hand, although machines are used to some extent. The beaten leaves are packed between tissue leaves of small books. Gold leaf may be rolled onto the sized surface from the tissue book. Generally, however, the gilder detaches the amount needed with a pointed tool, picks it up with a gilder's brush, and transfers it to the design. The leaf is held to the tip by static electricity, which the gilder generates by brushing the tip gently over his hair. When the gilding is completed, the leaf-covered area is pounced with a wad of soft cotton to burnish the gold to a high lustre. Leaf gold may be powdered by being rubbed through a fine-mesh sieve. Powdered gold is so costly, however, that bronze powders have been substituted almost universally. Metallic powders may be pounced on a sized surface with a soft material such as velvet or may be combined with a lacquer or with a chemical base and then applied as metallic paint.

heated to drive off the mercury. The panels of the *Gates of Paradise* in Florence, by the 15th-century sculptor Lorenzo Ghiberti, are a well-known example of gilded bronze.

PATINATION

Patinas on metals are caused by the corrosive action of chemicals. Sculpture that is exposed to different kinds of atmosphere or buried in soil or immersed in seawater for some time acquires a patina that can be extremely attractive. Similar effects can be achieved artificially by applying various chemicals to the metal surface, which is often heated to create a bond. This is a particularly effective treatment for bronze, which can be given a wide variety of attractive green, brown, blue, and black patinas. Iron is sometimes allowed to rust until it acquires a satisfactory colour, and then the process is arrested by lacquering.

ELECTROPLATING

The surfaces of metal sculpture or of specially prepared nonmetal sculpture can be coated with such metals as chrome, silver, gold, copper, and nickel by the familiar industrial process of electroplating. The related technique of anodizing can be used to prevent the corrosion of aluminum sculpture and to dye its surface.

OTHER FINISHES

The surfaces of metal sculpture can be decorated by means of numerous metalsmithing techniques—etching, engraving, metal inlaying, enameling, and so on. Pottery sculpture can be decorated with coloured slips, oxides, and

ANODIZING

Anodizing is a method of plating metal for such purposes as corrosion resistance, electrical insulation, thermal control, abrasion resistance, sealing, improving paint adhesion, and decorative finishing. Anodizing consists of electrically depositing an oxide film from aqueous solution onto the surface of a metal, often aluminum, which serves as the anode in an electrolytic cell. Plate properties such as porousness, abrasion resistance, colour, and flexibility depend on the type, concentration, and temperature of the electrolyte, the strength of the electrical current and the processing time, and the type of metal being plated. In the most common type of anodizing, which uses a 15 percent sulfuric acid bath, dyes can be introduced into the oxidation process in order to achieve a coloured surface. Aluminum that has been anodized and coloured in this way is used widely in giftware, home appliances, and architectural decoration.

enamels; glazed with a variety of shiny or mat glazes; and brought to a dull polish by burnishing.

Other materials have often been added to the surface of sculpture. The eyes of ancient figure sculpture, for example, were sometimes inlaid with stones. Occasionally—as in Mexican mosaic work—the whole surface of a sculpture is inlaid with mother-of-pearl, turquoise, coral, and many other substances.

CHAPTER FOUR

FORMS, SUBJECT MATTER, IMAGERY, AND SYMBOLISM OF SCULPTURE

A great deal of sculpture is designed to be placed in public squares, gardens, parks, and similar open places or in interior positions where it is isolated in space and can be viewed from all directions. Other sculpture is carved in relief and is viewed only from the front and sides.

SCULPTURE IN THE ROUND

The opportunities for free spatial design that such freestanding sculpture presents are not always fully exploited. The work may be designed, like many Archaic sculptures, to be viewed from only one or two fixed positions, or it may in effect be little more than a four-sided relief that hardly changes the three-dimensional form of the block at all. Sixteenth-century Mannerist sculptors, on the other hand, made a special point of exploiting the all-around visibility of freestanding sculpture. Giambologna's *Rape of the Sabines* (1579–83), for example, compels the viewer to walk all around it in order to grasp its spatial design. It has no principal views; its forms move around the central axis of the composition, and their serpentine movement unfolds itself gradually as the spectator moves around to follow them. Much of the sculpture of Henry Moore and other 20th-century sculptors is not concerned with movement of this kind, nor is it designed to be viewed from any fixed positions. Rather, it is a freely designed structure of multi-directional forms that is opened up, pierced, and extended in space in such a way that the viewer is made aware of its all-around design largely by seeing through the sculpture. The majority of constructed sculptures are disposed in space with complete freedom and invite viewing from all directions. In many instances the spectator can actually walk under and through them.

Henry Moore's *Large Reclining Figure* (1984), 20 1/2 feet (9 metres) long, is situated at Perry Green in Hertfordshire, England. People can walk beneath parts of the sculpture.

The way in which a freestanding sculpture makes contact with the ground or with its base is a matter of considerable importance. A reclining figure, for example, may in effect be a horizontal relief. It may blend with the ground plane and appear to be rooted in the ground like an outcrop of rock. Other sculptures, including some reclining figures, may be designed in such a way that they seem to rest on the ground and to be independent of their base. Others are supported in space above the ground. The most completely freestanding sculptures are those that have no base and may be picked up, turned in the hands, and literally viewed all around like a netsuke (a small toggle of wood, ivory, or metal used to fasten a small pouch or purse to a kimono sash). Of course, a large sculpture cannot actually be picked up in this way, but it can be designed so as to invite the viewer to think of it as a detached, independent object that has no fixed base and is designed all around.

Sculpture designed to stand against a wall or similar background or in a niche may be in the round and freestanding in the sense that it is not attached to its background like a relief, but it does not have the spatial independence of completely freestanding sculpture, and it is not designed to be viewed all around. It must be designed so that its formal structure and the nature and meaning of its subject matter can be clearly apprehended from a limited range of frontal views. The forms of the sculpture, therefore, are usually spread out mainly in a lateral direction rather than in depth. Greek pedimental sculpture illustrates this approach superbly: the composition is spread out in a plane perpendicular to the viewer's line of sight and is made completely intelligible from the front. Seventeenth-century Baroque sculptors, especially Bernini, adopted a rather different approach. Though some favoured a coherent frontal viewpoint, however active, Bernini is known to have conceived a work (the *Apollo and Daphne* [1622–25]) in which the narrative unfolded in details discovered as the viewer walked around the work, beginning from the rear.

The frontal composition of wall and niche sculpture does not necessarily imply any lack of three-dimensionality in the forms themselves; it is only the arrangement of the forms that is limited. Classical pedimental sculpture, Indian temple sculpture such as that at Khajuraho, Gothic niche sculpture, and Michelangelo's Medici tomb figures are all designed to be placed against a background, but their forms are conceived with a complete fullness of volume.

THE GREAT PHIDIAS AND THE PARTHENON SCULPTURES

The greatest name in Greek sculpture is that of Phidias (flourished *c.* 490–430 BCE). Under his direction the sculptures decorating the Parthenon on the Acropolis in Athens were planned and executed. Some of them may have been the work of his own hand. One of his masterpieces was the colossal statue of the *Athena Parthenos* at the Parthenon that was completed and dedicated in 438 BCE. The original work was made of gold and ivory and stood some 38 feet (12 metres) high. The goddess stood erect, wearing a tunic, aegis, and helmet and holding a Nike (goddess of victory) in her extended right hand and a spear in her left. A decorated shield and a serpent were by her side. Several copies have been identified from this description; among them are the *Varakion*, a Roman copy of about 130 CE, and a Hellenistic copy, from about 160 BCE, made for the main hall of the royal library at Pergamum.

Ancient writers considered Phidias' *Zeus*, completed about 430, for the Temple of Zeus at Olympia to be his great masterpiece; this colossal statue is now considered to be one of the Seven Wonders of the Ancient World. *Zeus* was seated on a throne, holding a Nike in his right hand and a sceptre in his left. His flesh was of ivory, his drapery of gold. The throneback rose above his head. Everything surrounding the figure, including the statues and paintings (by Panaenos), was richly decorated. The Olympian *Zeus* was about seven times life size (or 42 feet [13 metres]) and occupied the full height of the temple.

Both the *Athena Parthenos* and the Olympian *Zeus* have disappeared. Some of his great genius can be seen in the remains of the sculptures of the pediments and frieze of the

(CONTINUED ON THE NEXT PAGE)

(CONTINUED FROM THE PREVIOUS PAGE)

Parthenon. Many of them are preserved in the British Museum. They are known as the Elgin Marbles. Lord Elgin brought them from Athens in 1801–12.

The Parthenon sculptures are the greatest works of Greek art that have come down to modern times. The frieze ran like a decorative band around the top of the outer walls of the temple. It is 3 feet 3 1/2 inches (about 1 metre) high and 524 feet (160 metres) long. The subject is the ceremonial procession of the Panathenaic Festival. The figures represent gods, priests, and elders; sacrifice bearers and sacrificial cattle; and soldiers, nobles, and maidens. They stand out in low relief from an undetailed background. All are vividly alive and beautifully composed within the narrow band. The horses and their riders are particularly graceful. Their bodies seem to press forward in rhythmical movement.

Around the outside of the portico above the columns were 92 almost square panels known as the metopes. Each panel depicted two figures in combat.

In the east and west triangular pediments were groups of figures judged to be the world's greatest examples of monumental sculpture. The problem of composing figures in the triangular space of a low pediment was most skillfully solved.

The east pediment represented the contest of Athena and Poseidon over the site of Athens. The west pediment illustrated the miraculous birth of Athena out of the head of Zeus. The use of colour and of bronze accessories enhanced the beauty of the pediment groups.

RELIEF SCULPTURE

Relief sculpture is a complex art form that combines many features of the two-dimensional pictorial arts and the three-dimensional sculptural arts. On the one hand, a relief, like a picture, is dependent on a supporting surface, and its composition must be extended in a plane in order to be visible. On the other hand, its three-dimensional properties are not merely represented pictorially but are in some degree actual, like those of fully developed sculpture.

Among the various types of relief are some that approach very closely the condition of the pictorial arts. The reliefs of Donatello, Ghiberti, and other early Renaissance artists make full use of perspective, which is a pictorial method of representing three-dimensional spatial relationships realistically on a two-dimensional surface. Egyptian and most pre-Columbian American low reliefs are also extremely pictorial but in a different way. Using a system of graphic conventions, they translate the three-dimensional world into a two-dimensional one. The relief image is essentially one of plane surfaces and could not possibly exist in three dimensions. Its only sculptural aspects are its slight degree of actual projection from a surface and its frequently subtle surface modeling.

Other types of relief—for example, Classical Greek and most Indian—are conceived primarily in sculptural terms. The figures inhabit a space that is defined by the solid forms of the figures themselves and is limited by the background plane. This back plane is treated as a finite, impenetrable barrier in front of which the figures exist. It is not conceived as a receding perspective space or environment within which the figures are placed or as a flat surface upon which they are placed. The reliefs, so to speak, are more like contracted sculpture than expanded pictures.

The central problem of relief sculpture is to contract or condense three-dimensional solid form and spatial relations into a limited depth space. The extent to which the forms actually project varies considerably, and reliefs are classified on this basis as low reliefs (bas-reliefs) or high reliefs. There are types of reliefs that form a continuous series from the almost completely pictorial to the almost fully in the round.

One of the relief sculptor's most difficult tasks is to represent the relations between forms in depth within the limited space available to him. He does this mainly by giving careful attention to the planes of the relief. In a carved relief the highest, or front, plane is defined by the surface of the slab of wood or stone in which the relief is carved, and the back plane is the surface from which the forms project. The space between these two planes can be thought of as divided into a series of planes, one behind the other. The relations of forms in depth can then be thought of as relations between forms lying in different planes.

Sunken relief is also known as incised, coelanaglyphic, and intaglio relief. It is almost exclusively an ancient Egyptian art form, but some beautiful small-scale Indian examples in ivory have been discovered at Bagrām in Afghanistan. In a sunken relief, the outline of the design is first incised all around. The relief is then carved inside the incised outline, leaving the surrounding surface untouched. Thus, the finished relief is sunk below the level of the surrounding surface and is contained within a sharp, vertical-walled contour line. This approach to relief sculpture preserves the continuity of the material's original surface and creates no projection from it. The outline shows up as a powerful line of light and shade around the whole design.

Figurative low relief is generally regarded by sculptors as an extremely difficult art form. To give a convincing impression of three-dimensional structure and surface modeling with only a minimal degree of projection demands a fusion of draftsmanship and carving or modeling skill of a high order. The sculptor has to proceed empirically, constantly changing the direction of his light and testing the optical effect of his work. He cannot follow any fixed rules or represent things in depth by simply scaling down measurements mathematically so that, say, one inch of relief space represents one foot.

The forms of low relief usually make contact with the background all around their contours. If there is a slight amount of undercutting, its purpose is to give emphasis, by means of cast shadow, to a contour rather than to give any impression that the forms are independent of their background. Low relief includes figures that project up to about half their natural circumference.

INTAGLIO

Intaglio in sculpture is an engraving or incised figure in stone or other hard material such that all lines appear below the surface; it is thus the opposite of relief sculpture and is sometimes called "hollow relief." When the technique is used in casting, the design is cut in reverse into a plaster shell, which is then filled with the casting substance; the hollow impressions of the mold appear in relief on the cast. The most common use of intaglio is for engraved seals and precious stones, which are formed to produce a positive imprint when pressed into a plastic material such as heated wax. This form of intaglio has been used since antiquity, an example being Mesopotamian cylinder seals. It was used extensively on ceremonial arms and armour as well.

Technically, the simplest kind of low relief is the two-plane relief. For this, the sculptor draws an outline on a surface and then cuts away the surrounding surface, leaving the figure raised as a flat silhouette above the background plane. This procedure is often used for the first stages of a full relief carving, in which case the sculptor will proceed to carve into the raised silhouette, rounding the forms and giving an impression of three-dimensional structure. In a two-plane relief, however, the silhouette is left flat and substantially unaltered except for

the addition of surface detail. Pre-Columbian sculptors
used this method of relief carving to create bold figurative
and abstract reliefs.

Stiacciato relief is an extremely subtle type of flat, low
relief carving that is especially associated with the 15th-
century sculptors Donatello and Desiderio da Settignano.
The design is partly drawn with finely engraved chisel
lines and partly carved in relief. The stiacciato technique
depends largely for its effect on the way in which pale
materials, such as white marble, respond to light and
show up the most delicate lines and subtle changes of
texture or relief.

Donatello's stiacciato relief *Herod's Feast* (1423–27) is from a series
of reliefs that illustrate the life of John the Baptist and that embellish the
baptismal font in the Bapistery of San Giovanni in Siena, Italy.

The forms of high relief project far enough to be in some degree independent of their background. As they approach the fullness of sculpture in the round, they become of necessity considerably undercut. In many high reliefs, where parts of the composition are completely detached from their background and fully in the round, it is often impossible to tell from the front whether or not a figure is actually attached to its background.

Many different degrees of projection are often combined in one relief composition. Figures in the foreground may be completely detached and fully in the round, while those in the middle distance are in about half relief and those in the background in low relief. Such effects are common in late Gothic, Renaissance, and Baroque sculpture.

MODERN FORMS OF SCULPTURE

Since the 1950s, many new combined forms of art have been developed that do not fit readily into any of the traditional categories. Two of the most important of these, environments and kinetics, are closely enough connected with sculpture to be regarded by many artists and critics as branches or offshoots of sculpture. It is likely, however, that the persistence of the terms *environmental sculpture* and *kinetic sculpture* is a result of the failure of language to keep pace with events; for the practice is already growing of referring simply to environments and kinetics, as one might refer to painting, sculpture, and engraving, as art forms in their own right.

Traditional sculptures in relief and in the round are static, fixed objects or images. Their immobility and

immutability are part of the permanence traditionally
associated with the art of sculpture, especially monumental sculpture. What one refers to as movement
in, say, a Baroque or Greek sculpture is not actual
physical motion but a movement that is either directly
represented in the subject matter (galloping horses) or
expressed through the dynamic character of its form
(spirals, undulating curves). In recent years, however,
the use of actual movement, kineticism, has become
an important aspect of sculpture. Naum Gabo, Marcel
Duchamp, László Moholy-Nagy, and Alexander Calder
were pioneers of kinetic sculpture in modern times, but
many kinetic artists see a connection between their
work and such forms as the moving toys, dolls, and
clocks of previous ages.

There are now types of sculpture in which the components are moved by air currents, as in the well-known
mobiles of Calder; by water; by magnetism, the special-
ity of Nicholus Takis; by a variety of electromechanical
devices; or by the participation of the spectator himself.
The neo-Dada satire quality of the kinetic sculpture
created during the 1960s is exemplified by the works
of Jean Tinguely. His self-destructing *Homage to New
York* perfected the concept of a sculpture being both an
object and an event, or "happening."

The aim of most kinetic sculptors is to make
movement itself an integral part of the design of the
sculpture and not merely to suggest movement within
a static object. Calder's mobiles, for example, depend
for their aesthetic effect on constantly changing patterns of relationship. When liquids and gases are used
as components, the shapes and dimensions of the
sculpture may undergo continual transformations. The
movement of smoke; the diffusion and flow of coloured

water, mercury, oil, and so on; pneumatic inflation and deflation; and the movement of masses of bubbles have all served as media for kinetic sculpture. In the complex, electronically controlled "spatio-dynamic" and "lumino-dynamic" constructions of Nicolas Schöffer, the projection of changing patterns of light into space is a major feature.

The environmental sculptor creates new spatial contexts that differ from anything developed by traditional sculpture. The work no longer confronts the spectator as an object but surrounds him so that he moves within it as he might within a stage set, a garden, or an interior. The most common type of environment is the "room," which may have specially shaped and surfaced walls, special lighting effects, and many different kinds of contents. Kurt Schwitters's *Merzbau* (destroyed in 1943) was the first of these rooms, which now include the nightmare fantasy of Edward Kienholz's tableaux, such as *Roxy's* (1961) or *The Illegal Operation* (1962); George Segal's compositions, in which casts of clothed human figures in frozen, casual attitudes are placed in interiors; and rooms built of mirrors, such as Yayoi Kusama's *Endless Love Room* (1966) and Lucas Samaras's *Mirrored Room* (1966), in both of which the spectator himself, endlessly reflected, becomes part of the total effect.

Environmental art, in common with collage and assemblage, has tended toward greater concreteness not by making a more realistic representation, as naturalistic art does, but by including more of reality itself in the work, for example, by using casts taken from the actual human body, real clothes, actual objects and casts of objects, actual lighting effects, and real items of furniture. Plastic elements may be combined with music

ENVIRONMENTAL SCULPTURE

Environmental sculpture is an art form intended to involve or encompass the spectators rather than merely to face them; the form developed as part of a larger artistic current that sought to break down the historical dichotomy between life and art in the 20th century. The environmental sculptor can utilize virtually any medium, from mud and stone to light and sound.

The works of the American sculptor George Segal are among the best-known self-contained sculptural environments; his characteristic white plaster figures situated in mundane, authentically detailed settings evoke feelings of hermetic alienation and suspension in time. By contrast, the eerily realistic figures of Duane Hanson, an American influenced by Segal, are usually displayed in such a way as to partake of, contribute to, and indeed often disturb the given exhibition environment. Other notable sculptors of indoor environmental works include the American artist Edward Kienholz, whose densely detailed, emotionally charged works often incorporate elements of the surreal, and Lucas Samaras and Robert Irwin, also

(CONTINUED ON THE NEXT PAGE)

(CONTINUED FROM THE PREVIOUS PAGE)

Americans, both of whom have employed transparent and reflective materials to create complex and challenging optical effects in gallery and museum spaces.

The larger context of the natural and urban outdoors has preoccupied another group of environmental artists. The controversial "earthworks" of Robert Smithson and others frequently have entailed large-scale alterations of the Earth's surface; in one notable example, Smithson used earth-moving equipment to extend a rock and dirt spiral, 1,500

Robert Smithson's *Spiral Jetty* (1970) is a huge spiral extending 1,500 feet (460 metres) into the Great Salt Lake in Utah.

feet (460 meters) long, into Great Salt Lake in Utah (*Spiral Jetty*; 1970). The Bulgarian-born artist Christo and his wife, Jeanne-Claude, have involved large numbers of people in the planning and construction of such mammoth alfresco art projects as *Valley Curtain* (1972; Rifle Gap, Colorado). Their numerous "wrapped buildings" have been notable among urban environmental works of the past few decades.

and sound effects, dance, theatrical spectacles, and film to create so-called happenings, in which real figures are constituents of the "artwork" and operations are performed not on "artistic" materials but are performed on real objects and on the actual environment. Ideas such as these go far beyond anything that has ever before been associated with the term *sculpture*.

REPRESENTATIONAL SCULPTURE

Sculpture in the round is much more restricted than relief in the range of its subject matter. The representation of, say, a battle scene or a cavalcade in the round would require a space that corresponded in scale in every direction with that occupied by an actual battle or cavalcade. No such problems arise in relief because the treatment of scale and relations in depth is to some extent notional, or theoretical, like that of pictures. Then again, because a relief is attached to a background, problems of weight and physical balance and support do not arise. Figures can be represented as float-ing in space and can be arranged vertically as well as horizontally. Thus, in general, sculpture in the round is concerned with single figures and limited groups, while reliefs deal with more complex "pictorial" subjects involving crowds, landscape, architectural backgrounds, and so on.

THE HUMAN FIGURE

The principal subject of sculpture has always been the human figure. Next in importance in historical work are animals and fantastic creatures based on human and animal forms. Other subjects—for example, landscape, plants, still life, and architecture—have served primar-ily as accessories to figure sculpture, not as subjects in their own right, except as decorative elements within architecture or as precious carved witticisms such as those of the British wood-carver Grinling Gibbons. The overwhelming predominance of the human figure is due: first, to its immense emotional importance as an object of desire, love, fear, respect, and, in the case of anthropomorphic gods, worship, and, second, to its inex-haustible subtlety and variety of form and expression. The nude or almost nude figure played a prominent role in Egyptian, Indian, Greek, and African sculpture, while in medieval European and ancient Chinese sculpture the figure is almost invariably clothed. The interplay of the linear and modeled forms of free draperies with the solid volumes of the human body was of great inter-est to Classical sculptors and later became one of the principal themes of Renaissance and post-Renaissance sculpture. The human figure continues to be of central importance in modern sculpture in spite of the growth of nonfigurative art, but the optimistic, idealized, or naturalistic images of man prevalent in previous ages have been largely replaced by images of despair, horror, deformation, and satire.

DEVOTIONAL IMAGES AND NARRATIVE SCULPTURE

The production of devotional images has been one of the sculptor's main tasks, and many of the world's greatest sculptures are of this kind. They include images of Buddha and the Hindu gods; of Christ, the Virgin, and the Christian saints; of Athena, Aphrodite, Zeus, and other Greek gods; and of all the various gods, spirits, and mythical beings of Rome, the ancient Near East, pre-Columbian America, Black Africa, and the Pacific Islands.

Closely connected with devotional images are all of the commemorative narrative sculptures in which legends, heroic deeds, and religious stories are depicted for the delight and instruction of peoples who lived when books and literacy were rare. The Buddhist, Hindu, and Christian traditions are especially rich in narrative sculpture. Stories of the incarnations of Buddha—Jataka—and of the Hindu gods abounded in the temple sculpture of India and Southeast Asia, for example, at Sanchi, Amaravati, Borobudur, and Angkor. Sculpture illustrating the stories of the Bible is so abundant in medieval churches that the churches have been called "Bibles in stone." Sculpture recounting the heroic deeds of kings and generals are common, especially in Assyria and Rome. The Romans made use of a form known as continuous narrative, the best known example of which is the spiral, or helical, band of relief sculpture that surrounds *Trajan's Column* (c. 106–113 CE) and tells the story of the emperor's Dacian Wars. The episodes in the narrative are not separated into a series of framed compositions but are linked to form a continuous band of unbroken relief.

A detail of *Trajan's Column* (c. 106–113 CE), Rome, depicts the Roman emperor's victories beyond the Danube River. The marble column has a spiral band of low relief sculpture that forms a continuous narrative.

PORTRAITURE

Portraiture was practiced by the Egyptians but was comparatively rare in the ancient world until the Greeks and Romans made portrait sculpture one of their major artistic achievements. The features of many famous people are known to modern man only through the work of Roman sculptors on coins and medals, portrait busts, and full-length portraits. Portraiture has been an important aspect of Western sculpture from the Renaissance to the present day. Some of the best known modern portrait sculptors are Rodin, Charles Despiau, Marino Marini, and Jacob Epstein.

SCENES OF EVERYDAY LIFE

Scenes of everyday life have been represented in sculpture mainly on a small scale in minor works. The sculptures that are closest in spirit to the quiet dignity of the great 17th- and 18th-century genre paintings of Johannes Vermeer and Jean-Baptiste-Siméon Chardin are perhaps certain Greek tombstones, such as that of the *Stele of Hegeso* (410–400 BCE), which represents a quiet, absorbed moment when a seated young woman and her maidservant are looking at a necklace they have just removed from a casket. Intimate scenes of the people and their activities in everyday rural life are often portrayed in medieval and Egyptian reliefs as part of larger compositions.

ANIMALS

Animals have always been important subjects for sculpture. Paleolithic man produced some extraordinarily sensitive animal sculptures both in relief and in the round. Representations of horses and lions are among the finest works of Assyrian sculpture. Egyptian sculptors produced sensitive naturalistic representations of cattle, donkeys, hippopotamuses, apes, and a wide variety of birds and fish. Ancient Chinese sculptors made superb small-scale animal sculptures in bronze and pottery. Animals were the main subject matter for the sculpture of the nomadic tribes of Eurasia and northern Europe, for whom they became the basis for elaborate zoomorphic fantasies. This animal art contributed to the rich tradition of animal sculpture in medieval art. Animals also served as a basis for semi-abstract fantasy in Mexican, Maya, North American Indian, and Oceanic sculpture. The horse has always occupied an important place in Western sculpture, but other animals have also figured in the work of such sculptors as Giambologna, in the 16th century, and Antoine-Louis Barye, in the 19th, as well as numerous sculptors of garden and fountain pieces. Among modern sculptors who have made extensive use of animals or animal-like forms are Brancusi, Picasso, Gerhard Marcks, Germaine Richier, Anna Hyatt Huntington, François Pompon, Pino Pascali, and François-Xavier-Maxime Lalanne.

FANTASY

In their attempts to imagine gods and mythical beings, sculptors have invented fantastic images based on the combination and metamorphosis of animal and human forms. A centaur, the Minotaur, and animal-headed gods of the ancient world are straightforward combinations. More imaginative fantasies were produced by Mexican and Maya sculptors and by tribal sculptors in many parts of the world. Fantastic creatures abound in the sculpture produced in northern Europe during the early Middle Ages and the Romanesque period. Fantasy of a playful kind is often found in garden sculpture and fountains.

In the period following World War I, fantasy was a dominant element in representational sculpture. Among its many forms are images derived from dreams, the technological fantasy of science fiction, erotic fantasies, and a whole host of monsters and automata. The Surrealists have made a major contribution to this aspect of modern sculpture.

OTHER SUBJECTS

Architectural backgrounds in sculpture range from the simplified baldacchinos (ornamental structures resembling canopies used especially over altars) of early medieval reliefs to the 17th- and 18th-century virtuoso perspective townscapes of Grinling Gibbons. Architectural accessories such as plinths, entablatures, pilasters, columns, and moldings have played a prominent role both in Greek and Roman sarcophagi, in medieval altarpieces and screens, and in Renaissance wall tombs.

Outside the field of ornament, botanical forms have played only a minor role in sculpture. Trees and stylized lotuses are especially common in Indian sculpture because of their great symbolic significance. Trees are also present in many Renaissance reliefs and in some medieval reliefs.

Landscape, which was an important background feature in many Renaissance reliefs (notably those of Ghiberti) and, as sculptured rocks, appeared in a number of Baroque fountains, entered into sculpture in a new way when Henry Moore combined the forms of caves, rocks, hills, and cliffs with the human form in a series of large reclining figures.

There is nothing in sculpture comparable with the tradition of still-life painting. When objects are represented, it is almost always as part of a figure composition. A few modern sculptors, however, notably Giacomo Manzù and Oldenburg, have used still-life subjects.

NONREPRESENTATIONAL SCULPTURE

There are two main kinds of nonrepresentational sculpture. One kind uses nature not as subject matter to be represented but as a source of formal ideas. For sculptors who work in this way, the forms that are observed in nature serve as a starting point for a kind of creative play, the end products of which may bear little or no resemblance either to their original source or to any other natural object. Many works by Brancusi, Raymond Duchamp-Villon, Jacques Lipchitz, Henri Laurens, Umberto Boccioni, and other pioneer modern sculptors have this character. The transformation of natural forms to a point where they are no longer recognizable is also common in many styles of primitive and ornamental art.

The other main kind of nonrepresentational sculpture, often known as nonobjective sculpture, is a more completely nonrepresentational form that does not even have a starting point in nature. It arises from a constructive manipulation of the sculptor's generalized, abstract ideas of spatial relations, volume, line, colour, texture, and so on. The approach of the nonobjective sculptor has been likened to that of the composer of music, who manipulates the elements of his art in a similar manner. The inclusion of purely invented, three-dimensional artifacts under the heading of sculpture is a 20th-century innovation.

Some nonobjective sculptors prefer forms that have the complex curvilinearity of surface typical of living organisms; others prefer more regular, simple geometric forms. The whole realm of three-dimensional form is open to nonobjective sculptors, but these sculptors often restrict themselves to a narrow range of preferred types of form. A kind of nonobjective sculpture prominent in the 1950s and '60s, for example, consisted of extremely stark, so-called primary forms. These were highly finished, usually coloured constructions that were often large in scale and made up entirely of plane or single-curved surfaces. Prominent among the first generation of nonobjective sculptors were Jean Arp, Antoine Pevsner, Naum Gabo, Barbara Hepworth, Max Bill, and David Smith. Subsequent artists who worked in this manner include Robert Morris, Donald Judd, and Phillip King.

DECORATIVE SCULPTURE

The devices and motifs of ornamental sculpture fall into three main categories: abstract, zoomorphic, and botanical. Abstract shapes, which can easily be made to fit into any framework, are a widespread form of decoration. Outstanding examples of abstract relief ornament are found on Islamic, Mexican, and Maya buildings and on small Celtic metal artifacts. The character of the work varies from the large-scale rectilinear two-plane reliefs of the buildings of Mitla in Mexico to the small-scale curvilinear plastic decoration of a Celtic shield or body ornament.

Zoomorphic relief decoration, derived from a vast range of animal forms, is common on primitive artifacts and on Romanesque churches, especially the wooden stave churches of Scandinavia.

Botanical forms lend themselves readily to decorative purposes because their growth patterns are variable and their components—leaf, tendril, bud, flower, and fruit—are infinitely repeatable. The acanthus and anthemion motifs of Classical relief and the lotuses of Indian relief are splendid examples of stylized plant ornament. The naturalistic leaf ornament of Southwell Minster, Reims Cathedral, and other Gothic churches transcends the merely decorative and becomes superbly plastic sculpture in its own right.

SYMBOLISM

Sculptural images may be symbolic on a number of levels. Apart from conventional symbols, such as those of heraldry and other insignia, the simplest and most straightforward kind of sculptural symbol is that in which an abstract idea is represented by means of allegory and personification. A few common examples are figures that personify the cardinal virtues (prudence, justice, temperance, fortitude), the theological virtues (faith, hope, and charity), the arts, the church, victory, the seasons of the year, industry, and agriculture. These figures are often provided with symbolic objects that serve to identify them, for

example, the hammer of industry, the sickle of agriculture, the hourglass of time, the scales of justice. Such
personifications abound in medieval and Renaissance
sculpture and were until recently the stock-in-trade
of public sculpture the world over. Animals are also
frequently used in the same way, for example, the owl
(as the emblem of Athens and the symbol of wisdom),
the British lion, and the American eagle.

Beyond this straightforward level of symbolism,
the images of sculpture may serve as broader, more
abstruse religious, mythical, and civic symbols expressing some of humankind's deepest spiritual insights,
beliefs, and feelings. The great tympanums (the space
above the lintel of a door that is enclosed by the

Gislebertus carved the *Last Judgment* (c. 1135) in the west tympanum of
the cathedral of Saint-Lazare, Autun. The scenes were meant to scare the
faithful about being judged by God at the Second Coming of Jesus Christ.

doorway arch) of Autun, Moissac, and other medieval churches symbolize some of the most profound Christian doctrines concerning the ends of human life and humanity's relations with the divine. The Hindu image of the dance of Shiva is symbolic in every detail, and the whole image expresses in one concentrated symbol some of the complex cosmological ideas of the Hindu religion. The Buddhist temple of Borobudur, in Java, is one of the most complex and integrated of all religious symbols. It is designed as a holy mountain whose structure symbolizes the structure of the spiritual universe. Each of the nine levels of the temple has a different kind of sculptural symbolism, progressing from symbols of hell and the world of desire at the lowest level to austere symbols of the higher spiritual mysteries at its uppermost levels.

In more individualistic societies, works of sculpture may be symbolic on a personal, private level. Michelangelo's "Slaves" have been interpreted as Neoplatonic allegories of the human soul struggling to free itself from the bondage of the body, its "earthly prison," or, more directly, as symbols of the struggle of intelligible form against mere matter. But there is no doubt that, in ways difficult to formulate precisely, they are also disturbing symbols of Michelangelo's personal attitudes, emotions, and psychological conflicts. If it is an expression of his unconscious mind, the sculptor himself may be unaware of this aspect of the design of his work.

Many modern sculptors disclaim any attempt at symbolism in their work. When symbolic images do play a part in modern sculpture, they are either derived from obsolete classical, medieval, and other historical sources or they are private. Because there

THE TYMPANUM

The tympanum (plural: tympana) in Classical architecture is the area enclosed by a pediment, whether triangular or segmental. In a triangular pediment, the area is defined by the horizontal cornice along the bottom and by the raking (sloping) cornice along the sides; in a segmental pediment, the sides have segmental cornices. A pediment often contains sculpture, as at the Parthenon.

In Romanesque architecture, the tympanum constitutes the area between the lintel over a doorway and the arch above. During the 11th and 12th centuries in Europe, tympana over church portals were decorated with intricate and stylized relief sculpture.

A particularly popular subject for tympanum decoration was the Last Judgment. Typically, the figure of Christ appears in the centre of the composition, dominant in size and usually enclosed in a mandorla (an oval, nimbus-like form). At his right and left are the four Evangelists, sometimes represented or accompanied by their animal symbols. To the sides, smaller figures of angels and demons weigh sins of the resurrected dead, who are

(CONTINUED ON THE NEXT PAGE)

(CONTINUED FROM THE PREVIOUS PAGE)

ranked along the lowest and smallest section of the tympanum, directly above the lintel. Fine examples of Romanesque tympana may be seen at the abbey church of Saint-Pierre at Moissac, France, and at the cathedral of Saint-Lazare at Autun.

has been little socially recognized symbolism for the modern sculptor to use in his work, symbols consciously invented by individual artists or deriving from the image-producing function of the individual unconscious mind have been paramount. Many of these are entirely personal symbols expressing the artist's private attitudes, beliefs, obsessions, and emotions. They are often more symptomatic than symbolic. Henry Moore is outstanding among modern sculptors for having created a world of personal symbols that also have a universal quality, and Naum Gabo has sought images that would symbolize in a general way modern attitudes to the world picture provided by science and technology.

Examples of sculpture of which the positioning, or siting, as well as the imagery is symbolic are the carved boundary stones of the ancient world; memorials sited on battlegrounds or at places where religious and political martyrs have been killed; the Statue of Liberty and similar civic symbols situated at harbours, town gates, bridges, and so on; and the scenes of the Last Judgment placed over the entrances to cathedrals, where they could serve as an admonition to the congregation.

The choice of symbolism suitable to the function of a sculpture is an important aspect of design. Fonts, pulpits, lecterns, triumphal arches, war memorials, tombstones, and the like all require a symbolism appropriate to their function. In a somewhat different way, the tomb sculptures of Egypt, intended to serve a magical function in the afterlife of the tomb's inhabitants, had to be images suitable for their purpose. These, however, are more in the nature of magical substitutes than symbols.

CHAPTER FIVE

USES OF SCULPTURE

The vast majority of sculptures are not entirely autonomous but are integrated or linked in some way with other works of art in other mediums.

DECORATIONS

Relief, in particular, has served as a form of decoration for an immense range of domestic, personal, civic, and sacred artifacts, from the spear-throwers of Paleolithic man and the cosmetic palettes of earliest Egyptian civilization to the latest mass-produced plastic reproduction of a Jacobean linenfold panel (a carved or molded panel representing a fold, or scroll, of linen).

ARCHITECTURE

The main use of large-scale sculpture has been in conjunction with architecture. It has either formed part of the interior or exterior fabric of the building itself or has been placed against or near the building as an adjunct to it. The role of sculpture in relation to buildings as part of a townscape is also of great importance. Traditionally, it has been used to provide a focal point at the meeting of streets and in marketplaces, town squares, and other open places, a tradition that many town planners today are continuing.

GARDENS AND PARKS

Sculpture has been widely used as part of the total decorative scheme for a garden or park. Garden sculpture is usually intended primarily for enjoyment, helping to create the right kind of environment for meditation, relaxation, and delight. Because the aim is to create a lighthearted arcadian or ideal paradisal atmosphere, disturbing or serious subjects are usually avoided. The sculpture may be set among trees and foliage where it can surprise and delight the viewer or sited in the open to provide a focal point for a vista.

Fountains, too, are intended primarily to give enjoyment to the senses. There is nothing to compare with the interplay of light, movement, sound, and sculptural imagery in great fountains, which combine the movement and sound of sheets, jets, and cataracts of water with richly imaginative sculpture, water plants and foliage, darting fish, reflections, and changing

The water's play, reflections, and gushing sounds and the sculpture of the *Latona Fountain* (c. 1670), Chateau de Versailles, France, were meant to appeal to all the senses.

lights. They are the prototypes of all 20th-century "mixed-media" kinetic sculptures.

COMMEMORATIONS

The durability of sculpture makes it an ideal medium for commemorative purposes, and much of the world's greatest sculpture has been created to perpetuate the memory of persons and events. Commemorative sculpture includes tombs, tombstones, statues, plaques, sarcophagi, memorial columns, and triumphal arches. Portraiture, too, often serves a memorial function.

JEAN-ANTOINE HOUDON

Jean-Antoine Houdon (1741–1828) was a French sculptor whose religious and mythological works are definitive expressions of the 18th-century Rococo style of sculpture. Elements of classicism and naturalism are also evident in his work, and the vividness with which he expressed both physiognomy and character places him among history's greatest portrait sculptors.

Houdon began sculpting at age nine and underwent the long training prescribed by the

Académie Royale. In 1761 he won the Prix de Rome, and while in Rome (1764–68) he established his reputation with a large marble statue of *St. Bruno* (1767) and an anatomical study of a flayed man, *L'Écorché* (1767), which brought him immediate fame and served later as the basis for replicas widely used for instruction.

In 1770, two years after his return to Paris, he presented a reclining figure, *Morpheus* (marble version, 1777), as his reception piece for membership in the Académie Royale. He earned his livelihood, however, through portraiture; his sitters included Denis Diderot, Empress Catherine the Great of Russia, and Benjamin Franklin.

Houdon created four different busts of Voltaire in addition to the renowned seated figure at the Comédie-Française, for which the sculptor made first studies shortly before the death of the aged philosopher in 1778. Five weeks later, on hearing of the death of Jean-Jacques Rousseau, Houdon hastened to the philosopher's home at Ermenonville and took a cast of the dead man's face, from which he developed the bronze bust that is now in the Louvre. In 1785 Houdon crossed the Atlantic to carry out a commission for a statue of George Washington. Several weeks spent at Washington's home at Mount Vernon were sufficient for him to complete his studies,

(CONTINUED ON THE NEXT PAGE)

(CONTINUED FROM THE PREVIOUS PAGE)

which he took back to France. The marble statue, signed and dated 1788, was set up in the Virginia state capitol at Richmond in 1796.

Houdon modeled his sculptures in clay, although subsequent versions might be of marble, bronze, or plaster. A skilled technician in all of these mediums, Houdon either took full charge of repetitions or limited himself to finishing touches upon his assistants' work. He preferred retaining the toolmarks in his sculptures rather than polishing them out, choosing to suggest a sense of freshness in execution that accorded with his concern for a characteristic pose and for the effect of a direct and vivid glance.

COINAGE AND MEDALS

One of the most familiar and widespread uses of sculpture is for coins. Produced for more than 2,500 years, these miniature works of art contain a historically invaluable and often artistically excellent range of portrait heads and symbolic devices. Medals, too, in spite of their small scale, may be vehicles for plastic art of the highest quality. The 15th-century medals of the Italian artist Antonio Pisanello and the coins of ancient Greece are generally considered the supreme achievements in these miniature fields of sculpture.

GLYPTIC ARTS

Also on a small scale are the sculptural products of the glyptic arts—that is, the arts of carving gems and hard stones. Superb and varied work, often done in conjunction with precious metalwork, has been produced in many countries.

CEREMONIES AND RITUALS

Finally, sculpture has been widely used for ceremonial and ritualistic objects such as bishop's croziers, censers, reliquaries, chalices, tabernacles, sacred book covers, ancient Chinese bronzes, burial accessories, the paraphernalia of tribal rituals, the special equipment worn by participants in the sacred ball game of ancient Mexico, processional images, masks and headdresses, and modern trophies and awards.

This Chinese bronze *jia*, a vessel used for holding or heating wine and for pouring wine into the ground during a memorial ceremony, is from the Shang dynasty (17th?–11th century BCE).

CHAPTER SIX

THE HISTORY OF SCULPTURE

The history of sculpture commences with the ancient cultures that developed in prehistoric times. Throughout the centuries, sculpture has changed in many ways and can be categorized into innumerable periods and movements. Despite these diverse categories, each is an extension of or a response to sculpture from preceding times.

SCULPTURE AMONG EARLY PEOPLES

The earliest club wielded by the caveman was no great work of art, but it was sculpture of a kind. The gods that early peoples created out of their fear required a form as tangible as the club, though more complex. The earliest worshipers could not cope with abstract ideas of their gods. They had to see, touch, sacrifice to, and sometimes punish them.

In Polynesia and Peru, in southern France, New Zealand, Africa, and Mexico we find evidence that sculpture entered into every aspect of primitive life. Many of these early objects—whether intended for use or decoration—are fascinating in their strangeness and beautiful in their design. Modern artists, seeking new and vital forms of expression, have found a rich fountain of inspiration in these crude but serious efforts of early humans.

In the Americas sculpture thrived long before the arrival of Christopher Columbus. The Tarascans and Aztec of ancient Mexico and the highly gifted Maya of Central America rank high in pre-Columbian sculpture.

Among the most interesting finds in pre-Columbian sculpture are the archaeological remains near the town of Tula, Mexico—the ancient capital of the Toltec. Among the structures were a palace complex, temple pyramids, a

The columnar figures of Toltec warriors top the Pyramid of Quetzalcóatl at the Tula archaeological site in Mexico.

THE ARCHAEOLOGICAL SITE AT TULA

Tula, also called Tollan, was the ancient capital of the Toltecs in Mexico, and it was primarily important from approximately 850 to 1150 CE. Although its exact location is not certain, an archaeological site near the contemporary town of Tula in Hidalgo state has been the persistent choice of historians.

The archaeological remains near contemporary Tula are concentrated in two clusters at opposite ends of a low ridge. Recent surveys indicate that the original urban area covered at least 3 square miles (some 8 square km) and that the town probably had a population in the tens of thousands. The major civic centre consists of a large plaza bordered on one side by a five-stepped temple pyramid, which was probably dedicated to the god Quetzalcóatl. Other structures include a palace complex, two other temple pyramids, and two ball courts. Another large civic centre stands at the opposite end of the ridge.

The main temple pyramid and its associated structures epitomize the stylistic characteristics of Tula architecture. Though small, the pyramid was highly decorated. The sides of the five terraces were covered with painted and sculptured friezes of marching felines and canines, of birds of prey devouring human hearts, and of human faces extending from the gaping jaws of serpents. A stairway on the southern side led to a highly ornamented two-room temple at the summit. The front room was supported by four columns in the form of erect, stiffly posed warriors, each 15 feet (4.6 metres) high and adorned with a series of highly specific body ornaments and accoutrements representative of the Tula style. Attached to the southern base of the pyramid was another feature of Tula architecture–great colonnaded masonry hallways with flat roofs supported on scores of masonry columns.

Separated from the main temple pyramid by a narrow alley are the partial remains of what may have been the palace of the ruler of Tula. The excavated portions consist of three great halls. Each apparently had a low bench placed along the interior walls (with projecting thrones at the midpoints), a central sunken light well, and great numbers of columns for support of the flat wood and masonry roof.

In general, the art and architecture of Tula show a striking similarity to that of Tenochtitlán, the Aztec capital, and the artistic themes indicate a close approximation in religious ideology and behaviour. In fact, many scholars believe that the Aztecs' concept of themselves as warrior-priests of the sun god was directly borrowed from the people of Tula.

civic center, and a platform altar. Distinctively carved columns supported part of the main temple. Typical of these are two sculptures of warriors 15 feet (4.5 metres) tall and decorated with what may be ceremonial ornaments and dress of their time.

THE ART OF EGYPT

As far back as 5,000 years ago Egypt introduced a style that, with surprisingly little change, continued for almost 3,000 years. Rules for the making of statues were rigidly prescribed, as were social and religious customs. Religion was the dominant force in life on Earth and it required certain preparations for the life beyond.

Sculpture was entirely associated with the needs of religion and the gods or with the earthly rulers who were regarded as their representatives.

To symbolize the godlike role of the kings, they were represented as half-human, half-animal. The great Sphinx at Giza is the best-known example. To express their power and eternal life, they were carved in the hardest stone and in colossal proportions. The statues of Ramses II at Abu Simbel (now moved to southern Egypt) are examples.

Of the many treasures excavated in Egypt, the limestone head of Queen Nefertiti is one of the finest. The breath of life seems to animate the face. The painted, subtly modeled surface and graceful flow of neck and features create

This painted limestone bust of Nefertiti (c. 1350 BCE), queen of Egypt, is in the Egyptian Museum in Berlin, Germany.

a sense of startling realism. Sculpture flourished until Egypt was conquered by the Persians, Greeks, and Romans.

MESOPOTAMIA AND ITS ART

More than 4,000 years ago the valleys of the Tigris and Euphrates rivers began to teem with life—first the Sumerian, then the Babylonian, Assyrian, Chaldean, and Persian empires. Here too excavations have unearthed evidence of great skill and artistry. From Sumer have come examples of fine works in marble, diorite, hammered gold, and lapis lazuli. Of the many figures produced in this area, some of the best are those of Gudea, ruler of Lagash.

Some of the figures are in marble, others are cut in gray-black diorite. Dating from about 2400 BCE, they have the smooth perfection and idealized features of the classical period in Sumerian art.

Babylonian and Assyrian sculpture is impressive in its vitality, massiveness, and rich imagination. Huge fanciful lions or winged bulls with human heads stood guard at palace entrances. Inside, the walls were carved with scenes of royal hunting parties, battles, and festivities. In Persia too, especially at Persepolis, fine sculpture was produced.

AFRICAN SCULPTURE

Although wood is the best-known medium of African sculpture, many others are employed: copper alloys, iron, ivory, pottery, unfired clay, and, infrequently, stone.

Unfired clay is—and probably always was—the most widely used medium in the whole continent, but, partly because it is so fragile and therefore difficult to collect, it has been largely ignored in the literature. Small figurines of fired clay were excavated in a mound at Daima near Lake Chad in levels dating from the 5th century BCE or earlier, while others were found in Zimbabwe in deposits of the later part of the 1st millennium CE. Both of these discoveries imply an even earlier stage of unfired clay modeling. About the time of these lower levels at Daima (which represent a Neolithic, or New Stone Age, pastoral economy), there was flourishing farther to the west the fully Iron Age Nok culture, producing large, hollow sculptures in well-fired pottery, some of the stylistic features of which imply yet earlier prototypes in wood.

Copper-alloy castings using the cire-perdue ("lost-wax") technique afford evidence of great sculptural achievements from as early as the 9th century CE, when the smiths of Igbo Ukwu (in what is now Nigeria) were casting leaded bronze, which is highly ductile, and smithing copper, which is not. Some three or four centuries later, the smiths of Ife, seemingly unaware that unalloyed copper was not suitable for casting (or perhaps wishing to demonstrate their virtuosity), used it to produce masterpieces such as the seated figure in a shrine at Tada and the so-called Obalufon mask in the Ife Museum. In fact, zinc brasses were used more than unalloyed copper. The largest corpus of this work is from Benin, where zinc brasses were used almost exclusively. These copper-alloy castings, together with pottery sculptures (the traceable history of which goes back even farther), are the main evidence for the early history of sculpture in sub-Saharan Africa.

Wrought-iron sculptures are found in a number of traditions, mostly in West Africa, including the Dogon, Bambara, Fon, and Yoruba peoples.

Stone sculpture occurs in several separate centres, employing both hard and soft rock, but there is usually

A sculpture of a king's head from Benin, Nigeria, 15th century, was made from zinc brass using the "lost-wax" process. The sculpture memorialized an *oba*, or king, of Benin.

not much evidence of a development through time in a single place. Ivory is a highly prized medium in many parts of Africa. Its fine texture makes it suitable for delicate sculpture, while its rarity leads to its employment in many societies for items of great prestige.

African wood sculptures are carved with similar tools throughout the continent. An ax may be used to fell the tree, but an adz, with its cutting edge at right angles to the shaft, is used for the substantive work of carving. The skill achieved with this tool is astonishing to the Western observer. Thin shavings can be removed with speed and accuracy, creating a surface (especially when the form is convex) that shows slight facets that catch the light and add to the visual interest. More-intricate work is done with knives. A pointed iron rod heated in the fire may be employed to bore holes in a mask for attachment to the costume and to permit the wearer to see. The surface of the sculpture is sometimes polished with the side of a knife or sanded down with rough leaves. Details are commonly picked out by a method involving charring with a red-hot knife (as among the Ibibio of Nigeria), or the carving is immersed in mud to darken its surface before oiling (as among the Dan people of Côte d'Ivoire).

ASIAN SCULPTURE

Reports of the splendor of Asian art were brought to Europe by Marco Polo. By the 18th century Europeans not only possessed original ceramics, enamels, and furniture from the East but were adapting Asian designs and skills in their own products. Chinese Chippendale furniture and chinaware are examples. The art of Japan was brought into prominence in Europe in the mid–19th century in Paris by the Goncourt brothers, and it was Auguste Rodin who first gave public recognition in the West to the sculpture of India. In the latter part of the 19th century, when Western artists were seeking inspiration for a newer, fresher art, these sources, together with those of Africa and Muslim countries, provided them with rich material.

Sculpture in India was centered on the worship of Buddha and the three gods who form the trinity of Hinduism—Brahma, Vishnu, and Shiva. Although Siddhartha Gotama, the Buddha, lived in the 6th century BCE, it was not until the 1st century CE that the familiar statues of him appeared. The Gupta period, lasting from the 4th to the 6th century CE, produced some of the finest examples of Buddhist sculpture. From the 1st through 7th centuries CE, the Gandhara region, in what are now Pakistan and Afghanistan, produced many examples of Greco-Buddhist sculpture. The Hellenistic influence was introduced following the conquest of north India by Alexander the Great. To Shiva are dedicated the monumental rock-hewn temples of the period from the 5th to the 8th century. The equally majestic sun temples to Vishnu date from the 11th to the 13th century.

The Chinese were master craftsmen and produced fine sculpture, especially in bronze. Although bronze casting existed a thousand years earlier, it was in the Zhou period (1046?–256 BCE) that China developed the art to its peak.

This is evident in the great ceremonial vessels used by the nobility for ancestor worship. From tombs of the Han Empire (206 BCE–220 CE) have come a rich variety of clay figures of people, animals, and household utensils designed to make life comfortable in the next world. Other objects are wrought in bronze, inlaid with silver and gold, and elaborately ornamented with abstract and fanciful designs. Carvings in jade and bas-reliefs on tomb walls also reached a high degree of excellence.

One of the most magnificent archaeological finds of the century was the tomb of the Qin emperor Shihuangdi near Xi'an, China. In March 1974 an underground chamber was found containing an army of some 8,000 life-size terra-cotta soldiers of the late 3rd century BCE. Other nearby chambers contained more than 1,400 ceramic figures of cavalrymen and chariots, all arranged in battle formation.

Life-size terra-cotta soldiers were found in the tomb of Shihuangdi, the first emperor of the Qin dynasty (221–207 BCE), near Xi'an, China, in 1974. The clay figures were once brightly painted with mineral colours.

The prosperous Tang dynasty (618–907) developed Buddhist art to its highest level. Stone was a favourite medium for religious sculpture, and iron replaced bronze in the casting of figures. The glazed terra-cotta figures of this period are especially fine.

With the decline of Buddhism in the Song period (960–1279), Chinese sculpture lost its vigor. Nevertheless, interesting works continued to be produced, such as the Bodhisattvas. In Japan Buddhism and its art followed the Chinese pattern.

THE GLORIOUS SCULPTURE OF GREECE

The glory of Greece was its sculpture. The roots of Greek sculpture reach into the earlier cultures of Crete, Mycenae, and even Egypt. The figures of the 7th and 6th centuries BCE lack life and movement; their faces wear the frozen smile peculiar to archaic sculpture. Even so, these early craftsmen, whose names are lost with the temples they decorated, showed sensitivity to the qualities of marble and a superb sense of design. As if to make up for the lack of life in their statues, archaic sculptors sought naturalism by painting them.

Greek sculpture rose to its highest achievement in the 5th century BCE, when the spirit of Greece itself was at its height. Of the temples built in this "golden age" of Pericles, the finest was the Parthenon, dedicated to Athena, goddess of Athens. It was ornamented by the master of Greek sculpture, Phidias.

Phidias could not possibly have done all the marvelous sculptures of the Parthenon, and only here and there can one be sure of the master's own hand. The

Three Fates, designed to fit the triangular space of the pediment, are generally believed to represent the finest treatment of drapery in sculpture.

Two contemporaries of Phidias were Myron and Polyclitus. The works of these two men are known to us through Roman copies only, but in the *Hermes with the Infant Dionysus* by Praxiteles (born about 380 BCE) we have an original of idealized beauty.

The Aphrodite of Cnidus is a Roman copy of the Greek statue by Praxiteles, c. 350 BCE, which is now lost.

In the Louvre, in Paris, stands the famous *Venus de Milo*, found in 1820 on the island of Melos. The sculptor is unknown.

The same museum possesses the *Nike*, or *Winged Victory, of Samothrace*. The forward push of her body, with wings and draperies flying in the wind, recalls the Nikes, or goddesses of victory, that adorned the prows of ancient ships. The statue is dated between 250 and 180 BCE, in the late Hellenistic period,

PRAXITELES

Praxiteles (flourished 370–330 BCE) was the greatest of the Attic sculptors of the 4th century BCE and one of the most original of Greek artists. By transforming the detached and majestic style of his immediate predecessors into one of gentle grace and sensuous charm, he profoundly influenced the subsequent course of Greek sculpture.

Nothing is known of his life except that he apparently was the son of the sculptor Cephisodotus the Elder and had two sons, Cephisodotus the Younger and Timarchus, also sculptors. The only known surviving work from Praxiteles' own hand, the marble statue *Hermes Carrying the Infant Dionysus*, is characterized by a delicate modeling of forms and exquisite surface finish. A few of his other works, described by ancient writers, survive in Roman copies.

His most-celebrated work was the *Aphrodite of Cnidus*, which the Roman author Pliny the Elder considered not only the finest statue by Praxiteles but the best in the whole world. The goddess is shown naked, a bold innovation at the time. From reproductions

(CONTINUED ON THE NEXT PAGE)

(*CONTINUED FROM THE PREVIOUS PAGE*)

of this statue on Roman coins numerous copies have been recognized; the best known are in the Vatican Museum and in the Louvre. Another work that has been recognized in various Roman copies is the *Apollo Sauroctonus*, in which the god is shown as a boy leaning against a tree trunk, about to kill a lizard with an arrow.

According to Pliny, when Praxiteles was asked which of his statues he valued most highly, he replied, "'Those to which Nicias [a famous Greek painter] has put his hand'–so much did he prize the application of colour of that artist." To visualize the sculptures of Praxiteles, therefore, it is well to remember how much colour added to the general effect. Another ancient writer, Diodorus, says of him that "he informed his marble figures with the passions of the soul." It is this subtle personal element, combined with an exquisite finish of surface, that imparts to his figures their singular appeal. Through his influence, figures standing in graceful, sinuous poses, leaning lightly on some support, became favourite representations and were later further developed by sculptors of the Hellenistic Age.

following the death of Alexander the Great. Dramatic gestures and decorative detail replaced the quiet dignity and restraint of earlier days. In 1950 excavations on the island of Samothrace, on the site where the statue was discovered in 1863, uncovered the right hand of the figure. It was presented to the Louvre by the Greek government.

Under Alexander the Great's expanding rule, other Mediterranean countries and even Asia came in contact with Greek art. The spirit of Greek sculpture was to live again in Rome, in the Renaissance, and in several other periods about to be described.

FROM THE ROMANS TO THE RENAISSANCE

The Romans lacked the intellectual and aesthetic sensibilities of the Greeks. Their strength lay in military prowess, engineering, road building, and lawmaking. Their emperors required realistic portraits and triumphal arches to impress their own people and the subjugated nations of their far-flung empire.

The triumphal arches of the Emperors Titus and Constantine, adorned with scenes of victory and battle, have inspired similar efforts in Europe and America, from the Arc de Triomphe, in Paris, to the Memorial Arch of Valley Forge.

By the 2nd century CE, however, Rome and its sculpture both had lost their vigor. As collectors, copyists, and imitators of Greek sculpture, however, the Romans handed on to later generations the partial fruits of Greek labor.

CHRISTIANITY AND A NEW ART

In the 4th century the Roman Empire accepted Christianity as its religion. This meant a new kind of art. Sculpture, like painting, music, and philosophy, turned for inspiration to the church, and the church, faced with the need of interpreting the new religion for great masses of people, used the arts to good advantage. The vast majority of people could not read, and sculpture and painting became their books—as stained glass windows would a few centuries later.

Art was austere, symbolic, and otherworldly from about the 8th to the 12th century, the middle period of the Middle Ages. It was decidedly abstract, not realistic. Religious in subject matter, sculpture was closely related to church architecture.

Architecture in the Middle Ages developed two distinct styles: Romanesque and Gothic. Romanesque architecture, with the sculpture that decorated it, was born in Italy and derived its name from its similarity to the weighty monumental quality of Roman buildings. Late in the 12th century a new style, Gothic, was being developed in France, destined to spread to every Christian country and even as far as the Holy Land in the times of the Crusades. With its pointed arch and slender, lofty spires, it led to such architectural marvels as the cathedrals at Chartres, Bruges, Amiens, Reims, and others. Before yielding to Renaissance architecture in the 16th century, Gothic structures had been adorned with thousands of sculptured figures. The rounded arch, of Roman origin, identifies the Romanesque; the pointed arch distinguishes the Gothic.

TILMAN RIEMENSCHNEIDER

Tilman Riemenschneider (c. 1460–1531), master sculptor whose wood portrait carvings and statues made him one of the major artists of the late Gothic period in Germany, was known as the leader of the Lower Franconia school.

Riemenschneider was the son of the mint master of Würzburg, and the younger Riemenschneider opened a highly successful workshop there in 1483. As a civic leader he was councillor (1504–20) and burgomaster (1520–25). During the Peasants' Revolt (1525), he sympathized with the revolutionaries and was imprisoned for a short time, during which he temporarily lost his civic responsibilities and patrons.

His first documented work was the altar for the Münnerstadt parish church (1490–92), which was later dismantled. He had a continuous flow of commissions; his major work, the *Altar of the Virgin* (c. 1505–10) in Herrgotts Church at Creglingen, is a wood altar, 32 feet (10 metres) high, depicting the life of Mary. Riemenschneider employed numerous assistants on the massive monument, but he executed the dominant life-size figures himself. Other major works are *Adam and Eve*, stone

(CONTINUED ON THE NEXT PAGE)

(CONTINUED FROM THE PREVIOUS PAGE)

figures from the Würzburg Lady Chapel; the *Altar of the Holy Blood* (1501–05), in St. Jakob, Rothenburg; and the *Tomb of Henry II and Kunigunde* (1499–1513), in Bamberg Cathedral.

Although wood was his major medium, he also created pieces in marble, limestone, and alabaster. The sharply folded, flowing drapery on Riemenschneider's figures make his work easily identifiable. His later years in Kitzingen were spent restoring altarpieces and carving.

Tilman Riemenschneider carved the *Altar of the Holy Blood* (1501–05) for the church of St. Jakob in Rothenburg ob der Tauber, Germany.

The cathedral in the French town of Chartres, near Paris, is especially rich in fine craftsmanship. Its many carved figures are of the same stone as the columns and are part of them architecturally. Their gestures and expressions, like the simple pattern of their robes, seem frozen and unreal. And yet, in their very columnlike simplicity and rigid stiffness, they fulfill their architectural purpose admirably. Like the saints in the Byzantine paintings and mosaics of this period, their stylized, formal quality was set by tradition and by the church.

The Cathedral of Notre Dame in Paris shows the ingenuity and humor of medieval sculpture. Early in the Gothic period, sculptors adorned walls and roofs of churches with awe-inspiring monsters, symbolizing the devil's evil ways. Those extending from the wall as spouts for rainwater are known as gargoyles; those that simply served to scare people into mending their ways are called chimeras. Late Gothic sculptors created many fanciful figures.

The most distinguished sculptor who carried on the Gothic tradition in the 20th century was John Angel (1881–1960), an Englishman who worked in the United States. He created several figures for the Cathedral of St. John the Divine in New York City.

THE RENAISSANCE IN ITALY

The term *Renaissance*, meaning "rebirth," is used to describe the vigorous cultural activity of 14th- and 15th-century Italy and the revival of classical learning. Following Italy's lead, France and northern Europe also turned their interests from the rewards of heaven to the opportunities of their own world. In doing so they

found themselves akin in spirit to the Romans and Greeks before them. In their new love of life and search for knowledge they reached back a thousand years for every shred of instruction and inspiration. The Italians needed only to dig into the ground beneath them to find examples of the splendid sculpture of Rome.

It is an error, however, to assume that the artists of that exciting time meant merely to revive the past by imitating its achievements. Theirs was a new day demanding new expression, and they made this period in art the greatest since the Greek—a period in which exciting new styles and techniques began to appear.

The first sculptor to strike a new note was Nicola Pisano (1220?–84?). His carving on the pulpit in the Baptistery of Pisa resembles the carving on the marble sarcophagi in which the Romans buried their leaders. Nicola's son Giovanni (1247?–1314?) continued the trend toward greater naturalism and imbued his pupil Andrea Pisano (1270?–1348?) with the same ideal. Andrea brought the new style from Pisa to Florence. His 28 panels on the south doors of the Baptistery of Florence are bronzes of great skill and decorative appeal. They constitute one more important step toward emancipating sculpture from its restraint.

Two more sets of bronze doors adorn the Baptistery of Florence, both by Lorenzo Ghiberti (1378–1455). The first pair, designed for the north entrance, were so successful that he was commissioned to do the east doors as well. For 29 years Ghiberti and his assistants worked to produce the 10 panels devoted to biblical episodes. Finished in 1452 and brilliant in their gilding, the doors still astonish all who see them. Michelangelo pronounced them fit to be the "Gates of Paradise."

DONATELLO OF FLORENCE

Ghiberti's action-packed, deeply spaced compositions had brought relief sculpture to its highest level.
Among the Florentines who could appreciate this fact
was Donatello, the most gifted sculptor of the early
Renaissance.

Donatello (1386?–1466) was eager to depict the
spirit of adventure and freedom, the same spirit that
built new cities, discovered a new continent, and dared
to probe the secrets of the universe. His marble statue
of St. George is sturdy, confident, and just a bit defi-
ant, as befits the youthful champion of Christendom.
The bronze *David* has the easy grace of youth and
an elegance comparable to that of Greek sculpture.
Donatello's genius for embodying the spirit of the
Renaissance is expressed in *Gattamelata*.

Erasmo da Narni, nicknamed Gattamelata, was one
of those hired soldiers of fortune whom the Italians
called *condottieri*. They fought for pay and personal
glory and only rarely for an ideal. When Gattamelata
died in 1442 the Republic of Venice commissioned a
monument to his memory to be erected in the Piazza
del Santo in his native Padua. Because he was busy
with other commissions and because he was undertak-
ing the first equestrian statue since the days of imperial
Rome, Donatello took 10 years to complete this project.

The horse is almost bursting with the solid power of
a modern armored tank and yet is the embodiment of
all the gentle grace and rhythmic movement associated
with horses on parade. Gattamelata is erect and calm
with the untroubled poise of a conqueror. Looking at
this magnificent monument one can easily believe that

a sculptor can do more to make a general famous than all the general's victories put together.

Donatello's love for the delicate and the cheerful entered into even so formidable a work as *Gattamelata*, where the saddle is decorated with the playful figures of children, known in Italian as *putti*. The cantoria (singing gallery) that he made for the cathedral of Florence is one of Donatello's many expressions of his pleasure in depicting children in dance and song.

THE DELLA ROBBIAS

Donatello's younger contemporary, Luca della Robbia (1400?–82), also made a singing gallery for the same cathedral. Luca's first work incorporating terra-cotta was a tabernacle created for the church of Santa Maria Nuova in Florence in 1441 and later moved to Santa Maria in Peretola. In this work he used a glazed terra-cotta in three ways—as a background for marble reliefs, as reliefs against a marble background, and as a mosaic in combination with marble. Luca, his assistants, and his nephew Andrea evolved a method of enameling terra-cotta with a milky white glaze that was said to be a mixture of tin, litharge, antimony, and other minerals. This glaze they applied to figures placed against lovely blue backgrounds. The glaze was applied to the modeled clay figure that was then fired in a kiln. They produced many bas-reliefs of the Madonna and Child.

VERROCCHIO, PUPIL OF DONATELLO

Andrea del Verrocchio (1435–88) is the pupil in whom Donatello's genius lives on. Although he was distinguished as a painter, sculptor, silversmith, and architect, Verrocchio's fame rests largely on his equestrian statue of Colleoni.

Colleoni, another Venetian general, died 32 years after Gattamelata. Verrocchio's statue portrays him in his helmet and coat of mail, with head and body turned at angles and outstretched legs thrust into the stirrups. There are a dash and daring and even a note of arrogance in the posture. The powerful stallion seems every bit as proud as its master and looks resplendent in its ornamental trappings and curly mane. There are majesty and vitality in every muscle of its forward stride.

It is important to note that both the *Gattamelata* and the *Colleoni* were commissioned by the republic of Venice and not by the church. The church continued to call upon artists, as it had done for a thousand years, but it was no longer their sole patron. Families of merchant bankers had grown up with wealth and power enough virtually to control the city-states. The Medici family, for example, held sway over the city of Florence, and its patronage was eagerly sought by all artists. These families required the services of art to glorify their deeds.

THE GREAT MICHELANGELO

Lorenzo de' Medici (Lorenzo the Magnificent) delighted in the company of artists as well as in his rich collection of ancient manuscripts and antique sculpture. Ancient marbles, recently dug up, were placed in his gardens to be admired and to serve as inspiration for aspiring young talents. To these gardens and to the household of Lorenzo came a boy named Michelangelo Buonarroti (1475–1564), destined to create the most dynamic, robust sculpture in the modern world.

Michelangelo's sculptures on the Tomb of Lorenzo de' Medici in Florence depict the seated figure of Lorenzo, wearing a helmet, and reclining allegorical figures of sleep (Dusk) and waking (Dawn).

By the age of 26 Michelangelo was carving the heroic marble *David*, a triumph of anatomical knowledge. This may well be the finest statue ever carved. His Medici tombs, in the Chapel of San Lorenzo, Florence, are masterpieces of mortuary sculpture.

Probably his greatest works are the *Bound Slave* and *Moses*, both of which were designed for the tomb of Pope Julius II. Today the *Bound Slave* is in the Louvre and the *Moses* can be viewed at the basilica of San Pietro in Vincoli in Rome.

The marble *Moses* is justly regarded as the supreme example of skill and characterization. Troubled and disillusioned in his own long life, Michelangelo knew well how to carve into the face of *Moses* that look of sternness, sorrow, and amazement. What the great law-giver beheld among the Israelites on his descent from Mount Sinai is dramatically expressed not only in the face but in every agitated rhythm that courses through the beard, the limbs, and the drapery.

Michelangelo's achievements as a painter in the Sistine Chapel and as an architect for St. Peter's Church in Rome were enough to give him worldwide fame, but he preferred to sign himself "Michelangelo, Sculptor." As a sculptor he dominated the golden age of the Italian Renaissance.

The brilliance of the Renaissance in Italy was meanwhile spreading through Europe, and monarchs competed for the services of Italian artists and craftsmen.

CELLINI AND DA BOLOGNA

Benvenuto Cellini (1500–71) went to France at the invitation of Francis I. The exquisitely wrought saltcellar, made with gold and encrusted enamel, that Cellini made for this royal patron reveals his talents as a goldsmith. Large-scale sculpture he undertook later in his career, distinguishing himself with the bronze Perseus, which he made on his return to Florence. Cellini's description of the modeling and casting of this statue in his famous autobiography is in itself a masterpiece.

While some Italian artists journeyed to other lands, eager northerners came to Italy to study the new developments at their source. From Flanders came a young man who was to fall under the spell of Michelangelo and give the Renaissance in Italy its last great note of triumph.

Arriving in Florence in 1553, he remained in Italy to become known as Giovanni da Bologna, or Giambologna (1524–1608). *The Flying Mercury* is an extraordinary bronze of a figure in flight. His *Neptune Fountain*, at Bologna, is a work of vivid imagination and technical supremacy. Giovanni da Bologna concludes the great chapter of Italian sculpture of the Renaissance, but he also stands as a link between the Renaissance and the period described as the Baroque. In him the graceful elegance of the earlier Italian masters is secondary to the qualities characteristic of Michelangelo's followers: dramatic movement, exaggerated gesture, and technical skill.

THE BAROQUE IN SCULPTURE

Michelangelo had shown the way to express robust power with technical excellence. In his day these attributes of art were urgently desired by both church and state—the Roman Catholic church to bolster its prestige in the face of Protestant successes and the state to glorify its rising power. This trend carried over into the 17th century, when the zeal that built St. Peter's in Rome expressed itself in a renewed vigor wherever Roman Catholicism prevailed.

The leader of the Baroque movement was Gian Lorenzo Bernini (1598–1680), architect as well as sculptor. The series of 162 figures that surmounts his imposing colonnade in front of St. Peter's in Rome is only a part of the tremendous amount of work he did for the church. His fountains of Rome, including the *Fountain of the Four Rivers*, gave the Eternal City a new and lasting splendor. Typical of Bernini's style is his

Ecstasy of St. Teresa, where the overactive drapery and theatrical setting are designed to show off skill rather than to convey meaning.

SCULPTURE IN FRANCE

The Renaissance in France began about the time of Francis I (1494–1547). To his court were invited many Italian artists and architects, among them Benvenuto Cellini and Leonardo da Vinci. A little later, as the power of Italy waned and that of France rose, the ideas transplanted to the new country took deep root and blossomed into new life.

Even as early as the 15th century, Michel Colombe (1430?–1512?) had enlivened the old Gothic form with a touch of the new realism. But it was Jean Goujon (1515?–66?) in the 16th century who first achieved great distinction as a sculptor. With him the Renaissance in France came into full swing. His sculptured reliefs of nymphs decorating the *Fountain of the Innocents* are outstanding.

In the 17th century France responded to the influence of Bernini and the Baroque. The sculpture of Pierre Puget (1622–94) shows the exaggerations of the Bernini manner. François Girardon (1628–1715) worked under Puget for a time, and toward the end of the century became the leading sculptor in France. By the 18th century, French taste and skill had become the envy of Europe. The court at Versailles sparkled in regal elegance, and sculptors, along with painters and architects, were glorifying the gracious and the frivolous.

Sharing in this atmosphere of elegance, but free from frivolity, was Jean-Antoine Houdon (1741–1828).

Particularly successful as a portraitist, he worked in Rome, in the court of Frederick the Great of Prussia, and in America, as well as in his native France. His portrait busts show a searching study of character rather than a preoccupation with superficial charm so characteristic of his time.

While Benjamin Franklin was abroad courting the help of the sympathetic French for the American Revolution, he sat for the portrait by which he is known to many Americans. So pleased was the American patriot with Houdon's interpretation that when the U.S. Congress sought a sculptor for a full-length figure of George Washington, Franklin persuaded Houdon to cross the ocean. One of his figures of Washington now stands in the Capitol of Richmond, Virginia. Another is at Mount Vernon.

NEOCLASSICISM IN SCULPTURE

For all the interest in classical antiquity during and after the Renaissance, there had been no systematic study of classical remains until the brilliant and inspired work of the German archaeologist Johann Joachim Winckelmann (1717–68). His published writings on Herculaneum and Pompeii led to a new, impassioned interest in the ancient art of Greece and Rome. Artists now resolved to revive classical purity by adhering strictly to the style of original examples.

This movement, known as neoclassicism, began in the latter half of the 18th century and continued into the early 19th, when it gained political support through Napoleon's interest in Greek ideology. The leading exponent of this style in Italy was Antonio Canova (1757–1822). However correct in principle, his work remains cold in feeling, just as were the works of his followers in England, Germany, and Denmark.

In England John Flaxman (1755–1826) applied new classicism to public monuments and to the designing of classic motifs for Wedgwood chinaware. Germany's outstanding sculptors in this widespread tradition were Johann Gottfried Schadow (1764–1850) and Johann Heinrich von Dannecker (1758–1841). Bertel Thorvaldsen (1770–1844) of Denmark worked in Italy for about 40 years and won admiration for his rhythmic and rather chilly variations on the ancients' themes.

THE 19TH CENTURY

The formality and coldness of neoclassicism came as a reaction against the theatrical Baroque and against the florid Rococo, which flourished in 18th-century France. Moreover, the political atmosphere in which the new art operated was sympathetic to the reverence for the ancients. Napoleon saw himself as another Caesar. His minister of art, Jacques-Louis David, dictated that even furniture and dress be designed in classical lines. Gradually, however, artists returned to the life about them. François Rude (1784–1855) broke through classical restraint to create one of the world's most stirring relief compositions—the *Marseillaise* on the Arc de Triomphe, in Paris. Rude's pupil Jean Baptiste Carpeaux (1827–75) carried on the active, emotional themes.

Antoine-Louis Barye (1796–1875) meanwhile was producing a series of bronzes showing animals in dramatic, sometimes violent, action. His vigorous interpretations of nature contrast with the soft, studied mannerisms of the neoclassicists. Like many of Barye's works, his sculpture depicting a boa strangling a stag dramatizes a struggle between two animals; unlike the savage struggles of his jungle beasts, there is both power and pathos in this work.

SCULPTURE IN THE UNITED STATES

The first American sculptor of significance was the Philadelphian William Rush (1756–1833), who worked in wood. He left a fine full-size carving of George Washington as well as a vigorous self-portrait. His younger contemporaries, however, were studiously copying European examples of the neoclassical school in Italy. Horatio Greenough (1805–52) made an imposing figure of Washington in which he looks more like a half-dressed Roman emperor than the father of his country. Thomas Crawford (1814–57) decorated the Capitol in Washington, D.C. The statue of *Armed Liberty* surmounting the dome and the bronze doors are among his best works.

Henry Kirke Brown (1814–86) broke away from the sweet and sentimental in his robust and monumental equestrian statue of Washington in Union Square, New York City. The standing figure of Washington in front of New York City's Sub-Treasury Building on Wall Street by John Quincy Adams Ward (1830–1910) is dignified and monumental without remotely resembling a Greek god or a Roman emperor.

In the work of Augustus Saint-Gaudens (1848–1907), American sculpture reached a stature compatible with the country's growing wealth and prestige among nations. At a time when monuments to American Civil War heroes were being put up with more sentiment than sensitivity, Saint-Gaudens broke away from tradition and produced realistic works of great power.

Several other Americans came back from their studies abroad to establish sculpture on a high plane at home. Daniel Chester French (1850–1931) is well known for his figure of Abraham Lincoln in the Lincoln Memorial in Washington, D.C. Frederick MacMonnies (1863–1937), who studied in Paris

Daniel Chester French's *The Minute Man* (1875), the sculptor's first significant commission, is located in the Minute Man National Historical Park in Concord, Massachusetts.

DANIEL CHESTER FRENCH

Daniel Chester French (1850–1931) was a sculptor of bronze and marble statues and monuments whose work is probably more familiar to a wider American audience than that of any other native sculptor.

In 1867 French's family moved to Concord, Massachusetts. Though he had two unsuccessful semesters at the Massachusetts Institute of Technology (1867–68), he found a natural ability for sculpture and studied clay modeling with artist and fellow Concord resident Abigail May Alcott (of the famous Alcott family). In 1870 French briefly became an apprentice to sculptor John Quincy Adams Ward in New York City, and he also studied drawing in Boston with William Morris Hunt and anatomy with William Rimmer (1871–72). From 1874 to 1876 French worked in Florence, in the studio of American sculptor Thomas Ball.

It was from the town of Concord that French received his first important commission: the statue *The Minute Man* (dedicated in 1875), commemorating the Battle of Concord of 100 years earlier. It became the symbol for defense bonds, stamps, and posters of World War II. French's great and best-known marble, the seated figure of Abraham Lincoln in the Lincoln Memorial, Washington, D.C., was dedicated in 1922. In the intervening 50 years he created a vast number of works on American subjects. Among those are the equestrian statues of Gen. Ulysses S. Grant (dedicated 1899) in Philadelphia and Gen. George Washington (1900) in Paris; three pairs of bronze doors (1894–1904) for the Boston Public Library; the *Standing Lincoln* (1909–12), Lincoln, Nebraska; the statue of Ralph Waldo Emerson (dedicated 1914) in the Concord public library; the *Alma Mater* statue (1900–03) at Columbia University in New York City; and *The Four Continents* (1903–07) at the former United States Custom House in New York City.

In 1897 French bought a home in Stockbridge, Massachusetts, and named it Chesterwood. The estate, which included his home and studio, opened to the public as a museum in 1955 and became a site of the National Trust for Historic Preservation in 1968.

and with Saint-Gaudens, is known for his *Nathan Hale* in Manhattan's City Hall Park and *Horse Tamers* in Brooklyn's Prospect Park. George Grey Barnard (1863–1938) had his early training in the French Romantic-Impressionist school of Rodin but developed an individual power and imagination in such works as *Two Natures*.

In the meantime a small group of Americans were interpreting animal life and Native American lore. Paul Wayland Bartlett (1865–1925) is best known for *The Bohemian Bear Tamer*. With Frederic Remington (1861–1909), "cowboys and Indians" and their horses became the models for exciting bronzes. Gutzon Borglum (1867–1941), who is best known for his Mount Rushmore National Memorial, also produced a number of vigorous portraits, including the colossal head of Lincoln in the rotunda of the Capitol in Washington, D.C.

MODERN MOVEMENT

Sculpture in the 20th century became reestablished as a primary art, competing with, and even surpassing, painting. This renewal began with Auguste Rodin, whose *The Burghers of Calais* (1884–95) challenged centuries of tradition in public sculpture.

French sculptors such as Aristide Maillol (1861–1944) helped keep classic figure sculpture alive. But the tradition of sculpture concerned with the human figure was only one aspect of the modern movement. The great expansion of sculpture as a form of expression in the 20th century can be divided into three broad categories.

The figurative tradition was joined early in the century by one concerned not only with the human figure but also with the shapes of plants and other natural forms. Sculptors of biomorphic and figurative forms favour traditional methods—such as carving, modeling, and casting—and traditional materials—such as wood, stone, and bronze—that have been long associated with sculpture. Their works evoke the volume and mass of their medium and show the interplay between positive and negative space. Henry Moore's *Reclining Figure* (1963–65; Lincoln Center, New York City) provides a majestic illustration.

A second broad tradition, one with fewer connections to traditional sculpture, is called Constructivist after the Russian art movement in the early years of the Soviet state. The methods favored by Constructivists are those of modern industry such as welding, fusing, and cutting. The materials are not only those of heavy industry, such as steel, but also lightweight metals, glass, and modern materials such as plastics. Among the early masterworks of Constructivism was a model for a monument to the Third International, or Comintern, created in 1919–20 by Vladimir Tatlin (1885–1953).

A third tradition, associated with the Surrealist movement, consists of works that combine or transform objects or materials found in the everyday world, objects not made to be art. Artists who practice assemblage combine these everyday materials by gluing, nailing, and sewing. Others remake these objects so that they are seen differently— as in the oversized sculptures of Claes Oldenburg (born 1929) that re-create such common household items as a garden trowel. The boxes created by American artist Joseph Cornell (1903–72) combine such items as dolls, maps, and bottles to create mysterious miniature worlds.

Painters took a leading role in the development of modern sculpture. Four monumental *Backs* by Henri Matisse (1869–1954), done in low relief as wall sculptures, show how he simplified the forms of the human figure. Many artists worked within more than one tradition. Pablo Picasso (1881–1973), arguably the 20th century's most extraordinary artist, helped create or transform each of the sculptural traditions.

FIGURATIVE AND BIOMORPHIC SCULPTURE

In addition to Rodin's followers in France, artists who worked with the human figure include three Germans—Wilhelm Lehmbruck (1881–1919), who was associated with the expressionist movement in painting, Georg Kolbe (1877–1947), and Ernst Barlach (1870–1938). The figure of Lehmbruck's *Kneeling Woman* (1911) is distorted, the features and body made unnaturally long, recalling northern European sculpture of the Renaissance. The first generation of modern American sculptors included Gaston Lachaise (1882–1935) and the Warsaw-born Elie Nadelman (1882–1946), who created the elegant *Man in the Open Air* in about 1915.

Of artists aiming to simplify the figure, none was more influential than the Romanian-born Constantin Brancusi (1876–1957), who worked in France. A sequence—*Sleep* (1908), *Sleeping Muse* (1909–10), and *The Newborn* (1915)—shows how he progressively simplified the form of the head at rest. Such shapes as an egg, the wings of a bird, or a shell became elegant abstractions, finished in metal and stone to cool perfection; in rough-hewn stone and wood he created sculptures that have the presence of a tribal totem. A passionate wood-carver, he frequently carved prototypes for works later executed in other materials and produced numerous wood sculptures, often with a folk flavour.

The Italian painter and sculptor Amedeo Modigliani (1884–1920) was so impressed with the simple, stylized forms of African sculpture that he made creative use of it in his own work. The elongation of the head and the geometric simplicity of facial features in some of his works are influences from masks found in Africa. Modigliani was interested in creating a feeling of simple, solid elegance, touched with the mystic silence found in the stone carvings of the medieval Christian saints. Consequently he joined the two traditions in an original creation.

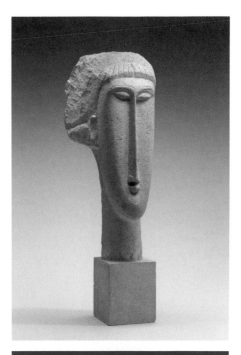

Amedeo Modigliani's *Head of a Woman* (1910–11) depicts a figure with a long neck and nose.

Alexander Archipenko (1887–1964), Raymond Duchamp-Villon (1876–1918), and Jacques Lipchitz (1891–1973) are among the most prominent of Cubist sculptors. Archipenko's *Walking Woman* (1912) shows one way that Cubism made possible a richer play of form and space in depictions of the human figure.

Cubism also opened the door to sculpture of everyday objects, as in Picasso's bronze *Glass of Absinthe* (1914). Artists active in Great Britain, including Jacob Epstein (1880–1959) and Henri Gaudier-Brzeska

(1891–1915), responded to Cubism with vigorous forms, as in Epstein's 1913 *The Rock Drill.*

Other early 20th-century art movements were reflected in sculpture. Umberto Boccioni (1882–1916) created works—for example, *Unique Forms of Continuity in Space* (1913)—that express the Futurists' desire to describe motion in art. The principal sculptural contributions of the Dada movement were the free-form reliefs and collages "arranged according to the laws of chance" by Jean (also called Hans) Arp (1887–1966). His 1920 wooden relief *Torso, Navel* is typical of his style.

Concern for the human figure and natural forms dominated sculpture in Great Britain from the 1920s until well after World War II. Henry Moore responded not only to traditional European art but also to the ancient sculpture of Mexico and Central America in his 1929 *Reclining Figure.* Barbara Hepworth (1903–75) abstracted forms from nature in such works as *Wave* (1943–44). This sculpture was hollowed out and variously perforated so that the interior space became as important as the mass surrounding it. Her rounded pieces seem to be the fruit of long weathering instead of hard work with a chisel.

THE CONSTRUCTIVIST TRADITION

The Russian Constructivists explored the sculptural possibilities of purely geometric forms and found ways to shape space. As such, their work was influenced by Cubism and Futurism. The art they helped to inspire has been more successful than the figurative, or object-related, traditions. Large sculptures based on abstract geometric forms have become, in the United States and elsewhere, a common form of artistic decoration in large office buildings and shopping centres.

During a visit with Picasso in 1913, Vladimir Tatlin saw such Cubist constructions as Picasso's sheet metal and wire *Guitar* (1912), which helped inspire Constructivism. Tatlin was convinced that space should be the sculptor's main concern.

Early Constructivist works—for example, the 1923 *Column* by Naum Gabo (1890–1977), made of glass and plastic as well as wood and steel—show how these artists were attracted to modern materials. They also show the closeness of their ties with architecture. After the movement was suppressed by the Soviet government in 1922, Gabo and his brother Antoine Pevsner (1886–1962) went abroad and helped spread the new ideas. Aleksandr Rodchenko (1891–1956) remained in the Soviet Union. His *Hanging Construction* (1920) is one of the first sculptures to define space by moving through it.

In 1928 Picasso began working in Paris in the studio of the Spanish sculptor Julio González (1876–1942), who developed the use of welded iron as a medium. Picasso also experimented with rods of welded iron, creating a type of sculpture that is similar to drawing in three dimensions.

An American working in Paris, Alexander Calder (1898–1976), also invented new forms. A maker of mechanical toys (and the son of a prominent American sculptor), he was inspired by the painters Piet Mondrian and Joan Miró to become an abstract artist. Marcel Duchamp saw his moving sculptures in 1932 and gave them the name "mobiles." Jean Arp then called the ones that had no movable parts and rested on the floor "stabiles."

OBJECTS AND ASSEMBLAGE

One of the century's most thoughtful and unpredictable artists was Marcel Duchamp (1887–1968). His 1913 *Bicycle Wheel* was the first "ready-made," an artwork made of ordinary objects. It was an old bicycle wheel mounted upside down on an ordinary kitchen stool. Duchamp's aim was not to please the eyes but to make the viewer think about what art is and can be. Duchamp made humour a significant factor in serious art. In 1915, for example, he exhibited a snow shovel on which he had written "in advance of the broken arm."

The Dada artists, whose art was a response to the brutality of World War I and an attempt to destroy traditional artistic values, found object sculpture a humourous way to express their revulsion. Morton Schamberg's *God* (about 1918), a carpenter's mitre box with a plumbing trap, and Man Ray's 1921 *Gift*, a flatiron with sharp tacks attached to the bottom, are classic Dada objects. The leading sculptor associated with Dada, aside from Jean Arp, was Kurt Schwitters (1887–1948). He created a one-man movement called Merz, a nonsense word like Dada. He made collages and assemblages from litter found in the streets and turned his entire house in Hanover, Germany, into a Merzbau. He continued to add to the Merz building for 16 years and later began work on Merzbau II in Norway and Merzbau III in Britain.

The Surrealist movement, which developed from Dadaism, continued to find inspiration in everyday objects. Instead of humour, the Surrealists made ordinary objects strange or disturbing, as in Meret Oppenheim's *Object* (1936), a fur-covered cup, saucer, and spoon. The art of non-Western peoples inspired artists such as Alberto Giacometti (1901–66), whose *Spoon-Woman* (1926) resembles a tribal cult object.

POSTWAR SCULPTURE

After World War II the center of the art world shifted to New York City. American painters soon led the way in developing new art concepts, but Europeans continued to dominate sculpture. The tragic events of the war seemed to require the classical art of the human figure.

Giacometti had left Surrealism behind in the mid-1930s and, after many years of study, began making sticklike sculptures. These figures, such as his 1947 *Man Pointing*, are so thin that they seem to be eaten away by the light around them.

Moore evoked the forms of rolling landscape, hollows, and hills in large public sculptures. Younger British artists—such as Elisabeth Frink (1930–93) and Eduardo Paolozzi (1924–2005)—and the French sculptor Germaine Richier (1904–59) also continued to develop prewar traditions. Italian figurative sculptors, such as Giacomo Manzù (1908–91) and Marino Marini (1901–80), made images, such as Marini's series of figures astride horses, that seemed to give tradition a new voice.

In the United States Calder refined his now-famous mobiles and created immense, but still playful, free-standing public sculptures. Another American, Isamu Noguchi (1904–88), worked for two years under Brancusi in Paris and traveled to Japan, where he studied traditional gardens. These influences are seen in his garden and *Fountain of Peace*, made for the United Nations Educational, Scientific, and Cultural Organization (UNESCO) in Paris in 1958.

American sculptor Isamu Noguchi is seen here in his outdoor workshop. He was known for using organic abstract shapes in his sculptures.

The artist who created a truly new American sculpture was David Smith (1906–65). His welded metal sculpture, inspired by the work of Julio González, was also shaped by his experience as a welder in a factory during World War II.

Hudson River Landscape (1951) has been called a "landscape drawing in space." He paid attention to the

ISAMU NOGUCHI

Isamu Noguchi (1904–1988) was an American sculptor and designer, one of the strongest advocates of the expressive power of organic abstract shapes in 20th-century American sculpture.

Noguchi spent his early years in Japan, and, after studying in New York City with Onorio Ruotolo in 1923, he won a Guggenheim fellowship and became Constantin Brancusi's assistant for two years (1927–29) in Paris. There he met Alberto Giacometti and Alexander Calder and became an enthusiast of abstract sculpture. He was also influenced by the Surrealist works of Pablo Picasso and Joan Miró. Noguchi's first exhibition was in New York City in 1929.

Much of his work, such as his *Bird C(MU)* (1952–58), consists of elegantly abstracted, rounded forms in highly polished stone. Such works as *Euripides* (1966) employ massive blocks of stone, brutally gouged and hammered. To his terra-cotta and stone sculptures Noguchi brought some of the spirit and mystery of early art, principally Japanese earthenware, which he studied under the Japanese potter Uno Jinmatsu on his first trip to Japan made in 1930–31.

(CONTINUED ON THE NEXT PAGE)

(*CONTINUED FROM THE PREVIOUS PAGE*)

Noguchi, who had premedical training at Columbia University, sensed the interrelatedness of bone and rock forms, the comparative anatomy of existence, as seen in his *Kouros* (1945). On another trip to Japan, in 1949, Noguchi experienced a turning point in his aesthetic development: he discovered "oneness with stone." The importance to him of a closeness to nature was apparent in his roofless studio.

Recognizing the appropriateness of sculptural shapes for architecture, he created a work in low relief (1938) for the Associated Press Building in New York City and designed *Chassis Fountain* for the Ford Pavilion at the New York World's Fair of 1939. He also made many important contributions toward the aesthetic reshaping of physical environment. His garden for the United Nations Educational, Scientific, and Cultural Organization (UNESCO) in Paris (completed 1958), his playground designs (all unrealized except the Noguchi Playscape, Piedmont Park, in Atlanta, completed 1976), his furniture designs (e.g., the glass-topped table designed for Herman Miller, 1944–45), and his fountain for the Philip A. Hart Civic Center Plaza in Detroit (completed 1979), among many other large-scale projects, won international praise. Noguchi also designed sculptural gardens for the John Hancock Insurance Company Building in New Orleans (completed 1962), the Chase Manhattan Bank Plaza in New York City (completed 1964), and the Israel Museum in Jerusalem (completed 1965) and stage sets for dance productions by Martha Graham, Erick Hawkins, George Balanchine, and Merce Cunningham. His career was celebrated with the first major retrospective of his work in 1968, held at the Whitney Museum of American Art in New York City.

Noguchi was awarded the Edward MacDowell Medal for outstanding lifelong contribution to the arts (1982), the Kyoto Prize in Arts (1986), and the National Medal of Arts (1987). The Isamu Noguchi Garden Museum, which opened in Long Island City, New York, in 1985, includes an outdoor sculpture garden and a collection of some 500 sculptures, models, and photographs. In 2015 the *New York Times* named Hayden Herrera's nonfiction work *Listening to Stone: The Art and Life of Isamu Noguchi* as one of its 100 Notable Books of 2015.

ideas associated with the objects in his sculptures and to their forms when combined, so both Constructivism and assemblage play a role in his work. In the 1960s he made sculptures that combine cubes, beams, and other basic shapes.

Other American artists followed the paths opened by Smith. Richard Stankiewicz (1922–83) combined industrial scrap. John Chamberlain (1927–2011) often used parts of wrecked autos. Louise Nevelson (1900–88) used scrap wood instead of metal, combining parts of demolished buildings in elegant works painted one overall color. Another American artist, Louise Bourgeois (1911–2010), sought to express personal emotional states in a variety of mostly large-scale forms.

In the 1960s there was further revolution. While artists such as the British Anthony Caro (1924–2013) continued to refine the discoveries of Smith, pop art once again inspired sculpture of everyday objects. Artists such as Jasper Johns (born 1930) and Andy Warhol (1928–87) re-created such things as a set of ale cans and a box of Brillo pads. Oldenburg re-created in vinyl such household items as light switches and bathtubs.

George Segal (1924–2000) and Edward Kienholz (1927–94) made entire environments, sometimes including a number of figures. Segal's figures were cast in plaster from living models. Kienholz's are realistically dressed but have fantastic and sometimes frightening heads that make his work more surreal.

A very different kind of sculpture then emerged— this new form tried to remove references to the everyday world, to be nothing, to represent nothing but itself. This minimal art can be seen as a kind of architecture that is free of the need to serve a client. Tony Smith's *Cigarette* (1966) is an early work in this style. Other artists associated with Minimalism include Robert Morris, Donald Judd, Sol LeWitt, and Carl Andre. In the 1980s Richard Serra (born 1939) made very large public sculptures of sheet steel, which caused much public debate.

In the 1970s art went in many other directions. One group of ambitious artists tried to make art that could not be contained by museums or galleries but was part of the environment. This land art resulted in some of the most impressive and thoughtful projects in American art history, including Robert Smithson's *Spiral Jetty* (1970), built into the Great Salt Lake, Utah, and the *Running Fence* by Christo and Jeanne-Claude, which ran across nearly 25 miles (40 kilometres) of California countryside in 1976.

Among European artists of the period, Joseph Beuys (1921–86) inspired and taught many of Germany's leading young artists. His sculptures were featured as part of performances. Other performing artists in both Europe and the United States made multimedia works that incorporated sound, video, and other untraditional elements within sculptural pieces.

In the 1980s more traditional materials again were favoured in painting, and this was true to some extent in sculpture as well. Artists turned to the past for inspiration. The human figure once again became a major element in work as different as that of Joel Shapiro, who made small-scale figures of short metal beams, and Tom Otterness, whose chubby little figures assume traditional poses or make up storytelling tableaux.

CHRISTO AND JEANNE-CLAUDE

Environmental sculptors Christo Javacheff (born 1935) and Jeanne-Claude de Guillebon (1935–2009) are noted for their controversial outdoor sculptures and monumental displays of fabrics and plastics.

Christo attended the Fine Arts Academy in Sofia, Bulgaria, and had begun working with the Burian Theatre in Prague when the Hungarian Revolution of 1956 broke out. He fled to Vienna, where he studied for a semester, and then, after a brief stay in Switzerland, moved to Paris and began exhibiting his works with the *nouveaux réalistes*. While working there as a portrait artist, Christo met Jeanne-Claude de Guillebon, whom he married in 1959. Jeanne-Claude was once described as her husband's publicist and business manager, but she later received equal billing with him in all creative and administrative aspects of their work. In 1964 the pair relocated to New York City, where their art was seen as a form of Arte Povera.

Christo's earliest sculptures were composed of cans and bottles–some as found and some painted or wrapped in paper, plastic, or fabric. Christo and Jeanne-Claude's first collaborative works included *Dockside Packages* (1961;

Cologne), *Iron Curtain–Wall of Oil Drums* (1962; Paris), and *Corridor Store Front* (1968; New York City). In 1968 they also completed a suspended 18,375-foot (5,600-metre) "air package" over Minneapolis, Minnesota, and "wrapped buildings" in Bern, Switzerland; Chicago; and Spoleto, Italy. Their monumental later projects included *Valley Curtain* (1972; Rifle Gap, Colorado), *Running Fence* (1976; Marin and Sonoma counties, California), and *Surrounded Islands* (1983; Biscayne Bay, Florida). In 1985 in Paris, they wrapped the Pont Neuf (bridge) in beige cloth. In a 1991 project, the couple installed 1,340 giant blue umbrellas across the Sato River valley in Japan and 1,760 giant yellow ones in Tejon Pass, California. Four years later they wrapped the Reichstag in Berlin in metallic silver fabric. *The Gates, Central Park, New York City, 1979–2005* was unveiled in 2005. Stretching across 23 miles (37 km) of walkway in Central Park, the work featured 7,503 steel gates that were 16 feet (5 metres) high and decorated with saffron-coloured cloth panels. *The Gates* was on display for 16 days and attracted more than four million visitors. In 2015 Christo installed *The Floating Piers* on Italy's Lake Iseo. Visitors "walked on water" for about two miles (3 km) on floatable cubes that were covered in yellow fabric and installed on the water.

Christo and Jeanne-Claude's huge, usually outdoor sculptures are temporary and involve

(CONTINUED ON THE NEXT PAGE)

(CONTINUED FROM THE PREVIOUS PAGE)

hundreds of assistants in their construction. Seen as they are by all manner of passersby, including those who would not necessarily visit museums, these works force observers to confront questions regarding the nature of art. As the scope of the projects widened, increased time was needed for planning and construction phases, the securing of permits, and environmental-impact research. For each project, they formed a corporation, which secured financing and sold the primary models and sketches. Most installations were documented in print and on film, and the materials that created them were sold or given away after the projects were dismantled.

Christo and Jeanne-Claude created *The Gates, Central Park, New York City, 1979–2005* as site-specific artwork.

Major artists of the 1980s explored other traditions. Nancy Graves (1939–95) welded cast objects in the tradition begun by Picasso and González. Alice Aycock's (born 1946) wooden "machines" recall the early creations of Constructivists such as Rodchenko.

Indian-born British sculptor Anish Kapoor (born 1954) used abstract biomorphic forms and rich colours and polished surfaces in his works. In *1000 Names*, created between 1979 and 1980, arrangements of abstract geometric forms coated with loose powdered pigments spilled beyond the object itself and onto the floor or wall. In the 1980s and 1990s Kapoor became recognized for his biomorphic sculptures and installations, made with materials as varied as stone, aluminum, and resin, that appeared to challenge gravity, depth, and perception. In the early 21st centrury Kappor's interest in addressing site and architecture led him to create projects that were increasingly ambitious in scale and construction. For his 2002 installation *Marsyas* at the Tate Modern gallery in London, for example, Kapoor created a trumpetlike form by erecting three massive steel rings joined by a 550-foot (155-metre) span of fleshy red plastic membrane that stretched the length of the museum's Turbine Hall. In 2004 Kapoor unveiled *Cloud Gate* in Chicago's Millennium Park; the 110-ton elliptical archway of highly polished stainless steel—nicknamed "The Bean"—was his first permanent site-specific installation in the United States. For just over a month in 2006, Kapoor's *Sky Mirror*, a concave stainless-steel mirror 35 feet (11 metres) in diameter, was installed in New York City's Rockefeller Center. Both *Cloud Gate* and *Sky Mirror* reflected and transformed their surroundings and demonstrated

Kapoor's ongoing investigation of material, form, and space.

American Jeff Koons (born 1955) managed to shock the art world with one audacious work after another, from displaying commercial vacuum cleaners and basketballs as his own art to making porcelain reproductions of kitsch objects to showing homemade pornography. In his early years Koons characteristically worked in series. To name only a couple, a series called *The New* (1980–83) included commercial vacuum cleaners and floor polishers in vitrines and his *Equilibrium* series (1985) consisted of cast bronze flotation devices and basketballs suspended in fluid. Koons was an early pioneer of appropriation, which called for reproducing banal commercial images and objects with only slight modifications in scale or material. In the first decade of the 21st century, he was best known for his fabricated objects from commercial sources—primarily inflatable pool toys and balloon animals—in highly polished and coloured stainless steel and for his paintings that layer and juxtapose various commercial and popular motifs.

Tara Donovan (born 1969), an American sculptor who makes sculptures from everyday objects (such as Styrofoam cups, Scotch tape, and toothpicks) on a large scale, is acclaimed for her site-specific installations. *Untitled (Plastic Cups)* (2006), which needs to be rebuilt each time it is exhibited, is stacks of millions of plastic cups that can be manipulated to fit the site. Her work has been linked to various Minimalist artists such as Carl Andre, Sol LeWitt, and Eva Hesse. One of Donovan's aims is to discover unanticipated qualities in everyday objects.

Sculpture, especially Western sculpture, has tended to be humanistic and naturalistic, concentrating upon the human figure and human action. Early in the history of the art there developed two general types: statuary, in which figures are shown in the round, and relief, in which figures project from a ground.

Sculpture in the ancient world of Greece and Rome and from the late Middle Ages to the end of the 19th century twice underwent a progressive development, from archaic stylization to realism; the term *progressive* here means that the stylistic sequence was determined by what was previously known about the representation of the human figure, each step depending upon a prior one, and not that there was an aesthetic progression or improvement. Modern criticism has sometimes claimed that much was lost in the change. In any event, the sculptors of the West closely observed the human body in action, at first attempting to find its ideal aspect and proportions and later aiming for dramatic effects, the heroic and the tragic; still later they favoured less significant sentiments, or at least more familiar and mundane subjects.

The pre-Hellenic, early Christian, Byzantine, and early medieval periods contradicted the humanist-naturalist bias of Greece and Rome and the Renaissance; in the 20th century that contradiction has been even more emphatic. The 20th century saw the move away from humanistic naturalism to experimentation with new materials and techniques and new and complex imagery. With the advent of abstract art, the concept of the figure had come to encompass a wide range of nonliteral representation; the notion of statuary had been superseded by the more inclusive category of freestanding sculpture; and, further, two new types appeared: kinetic sculpture, in which actual movement of parts or of the whole sculpture was considered an

Jeff Koons's *Puppy* (1992), an environmental sculpture of flowering plants that is 43 feet (13 metres) high, is on display at the Guggenheim Museum in Bilbao, Spain.

element of design, and environmental sculpture, in which the artist either altered a given environment as if it were a kind of medium or provided in the sculpture itself an environment for the viewer to enter.

With the emergence of the 21st century, some of the techniques and trends that were instrumental in the prior century continued to be pivotal. Assemblage, the incorporation of everyday objects into the composition, is among these methods. Jean Dubuffet coined the term *assemblage* in the 1950s and it may refer to both planar and three-dimensional constructions. Dan Levin and Michael deMeng are just two contemporary artists who create assemblages from discarded objects and give new life and meaning to these found objects.

Each period in sculpture is a link in the golden chain of creative achievement. If sculptors use historical examples and techniques to sharpen their vision, to deepen their insight, and to solve their problems, they use tradition creatively.

articulation The action or manner of jointing or inter-relating; the clarification of an architectural design by emphasizing certain parts of the structure (such as stairs, corridors, or floors).

bas-relief Also called low relief, sculptural relief in which the projection from the surrounding surface is slight.

biomorphic Related to, derived from, or incorporating the forms of living beings—used especially of primitive and abstract art.

chiaroscuro The arrangement or treatment of light and dark parts in a pictorial work of art.

chiastic pose A stance in which the body weight is taken principally on one leg thereby creating a contrast of tension and relaxation between opposite sides of a figure.

commission To give an order to (a person) for a work (as an artwork).

concave Hollowed or rounded inward like the inside of a bowl.

conservation The maintenance and preservation of works of art and their protection from future damage and deterioration.

contrapposto A position of the depicted human body (as in ancient Greek or late Renaissance sculpture) in which twisting of the vertical axis results in hips, shoulders, and head turned in different directions.

convex Curved or rounded like the outside of a sphere or circle.

diptych A picture or series of pictures (as an altarpiece) painted on two tablets connected by hinges.

fibreglass Glass in fibrous form used in making various products (as yarn and insulation).

flat relief Bas-relief in which projected parts have little or no modeling and the details are frequently marked by incised lines.

foreshortening A method of rendering a specific object or figure in a picture in depth.

glyptic The art or process of carving or engraving especially on gems.

high relief Sculptural relief in which at least half the thickness of the represented form is raised from the background.

homogeneous Of uniform structure or composition throughout.

inference The process of deriving as a conclusion from facts or premises; deduction.

intaglio An engraving or incised figure in stone or other hard material; specifically, a figure or design depressed below the surface of the material with the normal elevations of the design hollowed out so that an impression from the design yields an image in relief.

kinetic sculpture Sculpture in which movement (as of a motor-driving part or a changing electronic image) is a basic element.

lapidary Of or relating to precious stones or the art of cutting them.

maquette A usually small preliminary model (as of a sculpture).

matrix Something (as a mold) that gives form, foundation, or origin to something else (as molten metal) enclosed in it; a place or a surrounding or enclosing substance (as a rock) within which something (as a mineral) originates or develops.

metaphysical Highly abstract or difficult to understand; supernatural.

metope The space between two triglyphs (units each consisting of three vertical bands separated by grooves) of a Doric frieze (the part of an entablature between the architrave and the cornice) often adorned with carved work.

modeling Also spelled modelling, in sculpture, working of plastic materials by hand to build up form.

orientation In architecture, the position of a building in relation to an east-west axis.

patina A usually green film formed on copper and bronze by long exposure or by chemicals and often valued aesthetically.

perspective Method of graphically depicting three-dimensional objects and spatial relationships on a two-dimensional plane or on a plane that is shallower than the original (for example, in flat relief).

proportion The relation of one part to another or to the whole with respect to magnitude, quantity, or degree; balanced or pleasing arrangement; relative dimensions: size.

relief A mode of sculpture in which forms and figures are distinguished (as by modeling of soft material, hammering of thin malleable material, or cutting away the surface in a hard material) from a surrounding plane surface.

restoration The repair or renovation of artworks that have already sustained injury or decay and the attempted restoration of such objects to something approaching their original undamaged appearance.

round As in "in the round," in full sculptured form unattached to a background; freestanding.

sarcophagus (pl. sarcophagi) Stone coffin.

scrim A durable plain-woven usually cotton fabric.

submission The act of presenting something (as for consideration, inspection, or comment).

tensile Capable of stretching or being stretched: ductile.

vitrified Changed into glass or a glassy substance by heat and fusion.

BIBLIOGRAPHY

GENERAL WORKS ON SCULPTURE, METHODS, AND MATERIALS

Edward Lanteri, *Modelling and Sculpture: A Guide for Artists and Students*, 3 vol. (1965; previously pub. under the title *Modelling*, 3 vol., 1902–11), still an outstanding work on traditional methods; Jack C. Rich, *The Materials and Methods of Sculpture* (1947), comprehensive coverage of all except the most recent methods and materials; Wilbert Verhelst, *Sculpture: Tools, Materials, and Techniques* (1973), a wide-ranging survey with good coverage of modern materials; John W. Mills, *The Technique of Casting for Sculpture* (1967) and *Sculpture in Concrete* (1968), two useful technical handbooks; Trevor Faulkner, *The Thames and Hudson Manual of Direct Metal Sculpture* (1978), an informative work on a variety of historical and modern methods; Udo Kultermann, *The New Sculpture: Environments and Assemblages* (1968; originally published in German, 1967), a comprehensive account of these two recently developed forms of sculpture; Rudolf Wittkower, *Sculpture: Processes and Principles* (1977), an authoritative account of the interaction of techniques and aesthetics in the history of sculpture; L.R. Rogers, *Sculpture* (1969) and *Relief Sculpture* (1974), two books dealing with the principles and techniques of sculpture and their bearing on its appreciation as an art form. Nicholas Penny, *The Materials of Sculpture* (1993), treats the technical aspects, social history, and meaning of traditional sculpture materials.

Additional general works on sculpture include: Antonia Boström, ed., *The Encyclopedia of Sculpture* (2004). John Canaday, *What Is Art?* (1988). Judith Collins, *Sculpture Today* (2007). Frederick Hartt, *Art: A History of Painting, Sculpture, Architecture* (1993). Sam Hunter and others, *Modern Art: Painting, Sculpture, Architecture, Photography* (2005). H.W. Janson and A.F. Janson, *History of Art for Young People,* 6th ed. (2003). Martin Kemp, *The Oxford History of Western Art* (2002). Isabel Kühl, *50 Sculptures You Should Know* (2009). Joseph Manca and others, *1000 Sculptures of Genius* (2007). Don Nardo, *Sculpture* (2007). John Plowman, *Start Sculpting: A Step-by-Step Beginner's Guide to Working in Three Dimensions* (2004). Herbert Read, *Modern Sculpture: A Concise History* (2006). Robert Rosenblum and H.W. Janson, *Art of the Nineteenth Century: Painting and Sculpture* (1995).

GENERAL WORKS ON WESTERN SCULPTURE

An excellent general history of world art is Hugh Honour and John Fleming, *A World History of Art* (1982; U.S. title, *The Visual Arts: A History*), which examines sculpture in relation to the other arts. H.W. Janson, *History of Art* (1962; 2nd ed., 1977) is also recommended. Among books that discuss sculpture of many periods, Ruth Butler, *Western Sculpture: Definitions of Man* (1975) is unusually valuable. So, too, is F. David

Martin, *Sculpture and Enlivened Space* (1981). For the techniques of sculpture see W. Verhelst, *Sculpture: Tools, Materials, and Techniques* (1973) and Rudolf Wittkower, *Sculpture* (1977). The making of bronze sculptures, omitted from the latter, is brilliantly eluci-dated by Jennifer Montagu, *Bronzes* (1963, reissued 1972). Erwin Panofsky, *Tomb Sculpture* (1964), traces from ancient Egypt to about 1800 some of the major themes of one very important class of Western sculpture.

AFRICAN ART AND SCULPTURE

Recommended general accounts are Frank Willet, *African Art: An Introduction* (1971, reprinted 1985); J. Vansina, *Art History in Africa: An Introduction to Method* (1984); Werner Gillon, *A Short History of African Art* (1984, reissued 1986); and Robert Layton, *The Anthropology of Art* (1981), in part about Africa. Twentieth-century developments in contemporary art are surveyed in Ulli Beier, *Contemporary Art in Africa* (1968), Nkiru Nzegwu (ed.), *Issues in Contemporary African Art* (1998), Sidney Littlefield Kasfir, *Contemporary African Art* (1999), and Olu Oguibe and Okwui Enwezor (eds.), *Reading the Contemporary: African Art from Theory to the Marketplace* (1999).

The best account of sculptural traditions is still Eliot Elisofon, *The Sculpture of Africa* (1958, reissued 1978), with text by William B. Fagg; other visual media are discussed in John Picton and John Mack, *African Textiles: Looms, Weaving and Design* (1979); John Picton (ed.), *Earthenware in Asia and*

Africa (1984); Philip Allison, *African Stone Sculpture* (1968); Margaret Trowell, *African Design*, 3rd ed. (1971); Eugenia W. Herbert, *The Red Gold of Africa: Copper in Precolonial History and Culture* (1984); T.J.H. Chappel, *Decorated Gourds in North-Eastern Nigeria* (1977); and Roy Sieber, *African Textiles and Decorative Arts* (1972) and *African Furniture and Household Objects* (1980).

Studies of particular traditions are found in Warren L. d'Azevedo (ed.), *The Traditional Artist in African Societies* (1973); Paula Ben-Amos, *The Art of Benin* (1980); Daniel P. Biebuyck, *The Arts of Central Africa: An Annotated Bibliography* (1987), on Congo (Kinshasa), and *Lega Culture: Art, Initiation, and Moral Philosophy Among a Central African People* (1973); R.E. Bradbury, "Ezomo's Ikegobo and the Benin Cult of the Hand," *Man*, 61:129–138 (1961); Robert Brain and Adam Pollock, *Bangwa Funerary Sculpture* (1971); Eugene C. Burt, *An Annotated Bibliography of the Visual Arts of East Africa* (1980), concentrating on Kenya, Tanzania, Uganda, and the Makonde; Kevin Carroll, *Yoruba Religious Carving: Pagan & Christian Religious Sculpture in Nigeria and Dahomey* (1967); Herbert M. Cole, *Mbari: Art and Life Among the Owerri Igbo* (1982); Henry John Drewal and Margaret Thompson Drewal, *Gẹlẹdẹ: Art and Female Power Among the Yoruba* (1983); William Fagg, *Yoruba, Sculpture of West Africa* (1982); James C. Faris, *Nuba Personal Art* (1972); Everhard Fischer and Hans Himmelheber, *The Arts of the Dan in West Africa* (1984; originally published in German, 1976); Douglas Fraser and Herbert M. Cole (eds.), *African Art & Leadership*

(1972); Anita J. Glaze, *Art and Death in a Senufo Village* (1981); Robin Horton, "The Kalabari Ekine Society: A Borderland of Religion and Art," *Africa*, 33(2):94–114 (April 1963), *Kalabari Sculpture* (1965), and "Igbo: An Ordeal for Aristocrats," *Nigeria Magazine*, 90:168–183 (September 1966); Katheryne S. Loughran (ed.), *Somalia in Word and Image* (1986); John Mack, "Bakuba Embroidery Patterns: A Commentary on Their Social and Political Implications," *Textile History*, 11:163–174 (1980), and "Animal Representation in Kuba Art: An Anthropological Interpretation of Sculpture," *Oxford Art Journal*, 4(1):50–56 (November 1981); Katheryne S. Loughran et al., *Somalia in Word and Image* (1986); Simon Ottenberg, *Masked Rituals of Afikpo: The Contexts of an African Art* (1975); and Susan Mullin Vogel, *African Aesthetics* (1986).

Antiquities and rock art are discussed in Peter S. Garlake, *Great Zimbabwe* (1973) and *The Kingdoms of Africa* (1978); Jean-Dominique Lajoux, *The Rock Paintings of Tassili* (1963; originally published in French, 1962); J. David Lewis-Williams, *The Rock Art of Southern Africa* (1983); Henri Lhote, *The Search for the Tassili Frescoes: The Story of the Prehistoric Rock-Paintings of the Sahara*, 2nd ed. (1973); David W. Phillipson, *African Archaeology* (1985); Thurston Shaw, *Nigeria: Its Archaeology and Early History* (1978) and *Unearthing Igbo-Ukwu: Archaeological Discoveries in Eastern Nigeria* (1977); Patricia Vinnicombe, *People of the Eland: Rock Paintings of the Drakensberg Bushmen as a Reflection of Their Life and Thought* (1976); and A.R. Willcox, *The Rock Art of Africa* (1984).

CONSERVATION AND RESTORATION OF SCULPTURE

General issues related to sculpture are addressed in Soprintendenza Alle Gallerie di Bologna, *La conservazione delle sculture all'aperto* (1971); Norman Brommelle, Garry Thomson, and Perry Smith (eds.), *Conservation Within Historic Buildings* (1980); Norman Brommelle and Garry Thomson (eds.), *Science and Technology in the Service of Conservation: Preprints of the Contributions to the Washington Congress, 3–9 September 1982* (1982); and Norman Brommelle et al. (eds.), *Adhesives and Consolidants: Preprints of the Contributions to the Paris Congress, 2–8 September 1984* (1984). Stone sculpture is examined in *Deterioration and Preservation of Stones: Proceedings of the 3rd International Congress, 1979* (1979); Giovanni G. Amoroso and Vasco Fassina, *Stone Decay and Conservation: Atmospheric Pollution, Cleaning, Consolidation, and Protection* (1983); John Ashurst and Francis G. Dimes (eds.), *Conservation of Building and Decorative Stone*, 2 vol. (1990, reissued 2 vol. in 1, 1998); C.A. Price, *Stone Conservation: An Overview of Current Research* (1996); and Josef Riederer (ed.), *Proceedings of the 8th International Congress on Deterioration and Conservation of Stone*, 3 vol. (1996). Good sources on metal sculpture are David A. Scott, Jerry Podany, and Brian B. Considine (eds.), *Ancient & Historic Metals: Conservation and Scientific Research* (1994); Terry Drayman-Weisser (ed.), *Gilded Metals: History, Technology* and Conservation (2000); and E. Slater and N. Tennent (eds.), The Conservation and Restoration of Metals: Proceedings from the SSCR [Scottish Society for Conservation-Restoration] Symposium Held in Edinburgh, 30–31 March, 1979 (1979). Wood, as well as stone, is examined in Preprints of the Contributions to the New York Conference on Conservation of Stone and Wooden Objects, 1970, 2nd ed., 2 vol. (1971). See also Jackie Heuman (ed.), Material Matters: The Conservation of Modern Sculpture (1999).

DANIEL CHESTER FRENCH

Margaret French Cresson, Journey into Fame: The Life of Daniel Chester French (1947) is an early biography by his sculptor daughter. Michael Richman, Daniel Chester French: An American Sculptor (1976) is an exhibition catalog. Ernest Goldstein, The Statue Abraham Lincoln: A Masterpiece by Daniel Chester French (1997) discusses French's best-known work, situated in the Lincoln Memorial, Washington, D.C.

ISAMU NOGUCHI

Exhibition catalogues include Nancy Grove and Diane Botnick, The Sculpture of Isamu Noguchi, 1924–1979 (1980), and Valerie J. Fletcher, Isamu Noguchi: Master Sculptor (2004). Ana Maria Torres, Isamu Noguchi: A Study of Space (2000), with a foreword by Shoji Sadao, discusses and illustrates the artist's public works. Dore Ashton, *Noguchi East and West* (1992), and Masayo Duus, *The Life of Isamu Noguchi: Journey Without Borders*, trans. by Peter Duus (2007; originally published in Japanese), are biographies. A scholarly analysis of Noguchi, his art, and his political activism incited by World War II is Amy Lyford, *Isamu Noguchi's Modernism: Negotiating Race, Labor, and Nation, 1930–1950* (2013).

INDEX

A

Africa, sculpture in early, 10, 25, 27, 67, 72, 106, 107, 131–134, 135
animals, 33, 109–110
anodizing, 87, 88
Aphrodite of Cnidus, 139
Apollo and Daphne, 92
Archipenko, Alexander, 163
armatures, 70, 71
Arp, Jean, 164, 165, 166
assemblage, 73–75, 166–167, 172, 181

B

Barlach, Ernst, 25
Baroque sculpture, 6, 10, 91, 101, 112, 152–153, 155
Bartlett, Paul Wayland, 160
Barye, Antoine-Louis, 110, 155–156
Bernini, Gian Lorenzo, 6, 10, 16, 91, 92, 152–153
Beuys, Joseph, 173
Bicycle Wheel, 166
biomorphic sculpture, 29, 161, 162–164, 177
Bohemian Bear Tamer, The, 160
Bologna, Giovanni da, 89, 110, 151–152

Brancusi, Constantin, 1, 110, 112, 162
Brown, Henry Kirke, 156

C

Calder, Alexander, 101, 165, 167, 169
Canova, Antonio, 23, 155
carving
  techniques, 63–65
  tools, 65, 67–69
casting
  general techniques, 70–72
  reproduction, 78–79
cathedrals, 5, 10, 114, 118, 142, 144, 145
Cellini, Benvenuto, 151, 153
chiaroscuro, 5
Chinese sculpture, 25, 27, 31, 54, 85, 106, 110, 125, 134, 135–137
Christo, 105, 173, 174–176
ciment fondu, 39
clay, history of use in sculpture, 27, 31–36
Cloud Gate, 177
Colleoni, 149
constructed sculpture
  techniques, 75
Constructivism, 161, 164–165, 172, 177
contrapposto, 9–10
Cornell, Joseph, 161

craftsman, sculptor as, 58–61
Cubi, 30

D

Dadaism, 101, 164, 166
David, 10, 150
decorative sculpture, 113–114
Degas, Edgar, 16
della Robbia family, 34, 36, 148
designer, sculptor as, 58–61
devotional sculpture, 107
Donatello, 10, 24, 35, 59, 95, 99, 147–148
Donovan, Tate, 178
Duchamp, Marcel, 101, 165, 166

E

early peoples, sculpture of, 126–130
earthworks, 104–105, 173
Ecstasy of St. Theresa, 16, 153
Egypt, sculpture in early, 1, 5, 16, 18, 65, 69, 95, 97, 109, 110, 119, 120, 130–131, 137
electroplating, 87
environmental sculpture, 102–105, 173, 181
Equilibrium, 178

everyday life, as subject of sculpture, 109

F

fantasy, as subject of sculpture, 110–111
fibreglass, 38, 39–40, 57, 69, 71, 74, 79
files, 67–68
foreshortening, 12, 13
found objects, 74, 161, 166
Fountain of Peace, 167
France, Renaissance sculpture in, 153–154
French, Daniel Chester, 157, 158–159

G

Gabo, Naum, 3, 101, 113, 118, 165
Gattamelata, 147–148, 149
Ghiberti, Lorenzo, 87, 95, 111, 146, 147
Giacometti, Alberto, 167, 169
Gibbings, Grinling, 106, 111
gilding, history of use, 6, 84–87
Gothic sculpture, 5, 7, 92, 100, 114, 142, 143, 145
Goujon, Jean, 153
Greece, sculpture in, 5, 8, 9, 10, 12, 16, 18, 23, 27, 32, 34, 36, 83, 96, 101,

106, 107, 109, 111,
124, 137–141, 146,
154, 179

H

Hanson, Duane, 103
Hepworth, Barbara, 3, 113,
164
"Homage to New York," 101
Houdon, Jean-Antoine, 35,
122–124, 153–154
human figure, 3, 14, 106–
108, 162–164

I

Indian sculpture, 4, 5, 10, 12,
26, 27, 72, 92, 96, 97,
106, 107, 111, 114, 135
indirect carving, 64–65
intaglio, 97, 98
Irwin, Robert, 103
Italy, Renaissance sculpture
in, 5, 9, 14, 18, 23, 36,
95, 145–152
ivory, history of use in sculpture, 6, 36–37, 43

J

Jeanne-Claude, 105, 173,
174–176
Judd, Donald, 61, 76, 113,
173

K

Kapoor, Anish, 177–178
Kienholz, Edward, 42, 102,
103, 172
kinetic sculpture, 100, 101,
102, 122, 180
Koons, Jeff, 178
Kusama, Yayoi, 102

L

Lemoyne, Jean-Baptiste, 35
lost-pattern process, 80, 81
lost-wax process, 40, 72,
77–78, 79, 80, 81

M

Maillol, Aristide, 10, 160
marble, characteristics of and
history of use, 20–23
Mesopotamia, 131
metal
conservation and restora-
tion of, 51–52, 54
direct metal sculpture
techniques, 75–76
history of use in sculpture,
26–27
Michelangelo, 8, 10, 16, 18,
23, 60, 92, 116, 146,
149–151, 152
Middle Ages, sculpture
during the, 5, 27, 36, 38,
107, 111, 116, 142–
145, 179

Minute Man, The, 158
modeling
    for casting, 70–72
    characteristics of modeled
        sculpture, 73
    general techniques, 69–70
    for pottery, 72
modern sculpture, 100–102,
    105, 160–167
Modigliani, Amedeo, 163
Moholy-Nagy, László, 101
molding, techniques, 78–81
Moore, Henry, 3, 25, 60, 90,
    112, 118, 161, 164
Morpheus, 123
Moses, 150–151

N

narrative sculpture,
    107–108
neoclassical sculpture,
    154–155, 156
19th century sculpture,
    155–160
Noguchi, Isamu, 167,
    169–171
nonrepresentational sculp-
    ture, 112–113

O

Object, 166
Oldenburg, Claes, 42, 112,
    161, 172
Oppenheim, Meret, 166

P

painting, as finishing tech-
    nique, 83–84
Panofsky, Erwin, 7, 188
papier-mâché, 40, 41
Parthenon, 18, 92–95, 137
patination, 87
Pevsner, Antoine, 3, 113,
    165
Phidias, 60, 92, 93, 137
Picasso, Pablo, 16, 29, 110,
    162, 163, 165, 169, 177
Pisanello, Antonio, 16, 124
Pisano, Nicola, 146
plaster of paris, 37–39
pointing, 81–82
polishing, 82–83
portraiture, 109
postwar sculpture, 167–178
Praxiteles, 9, 12, 139–140
primary structures, 61
Puget, Pierre, 153

R

Reclining Figure, 161, 164
relief sculpture, design
    principles of, 95–100
Renaissance sculpture, 5, 9,
    14, 18, 23, 36, 38, 61,
    72, 95, 100, 107, 109,
    111, 115, 145–154,
    179
repoussé, 58
representational sculpture,
    105–112

Riemenschneider, Tilman, 143–144
Rococo sculpture, 122, 155
Rodin, Auguste, 12, 59, 64, 109, 135, 160, 162
Romanesque sculpture, 7, 111, 114, 117, 118, 142
Roman sculpture, 27, 34, 107–108, 109, 111, 141–142, 146, 154, 179

S

Saint-Gaudens, Augustus, 156–157, 160
Samaras, Lucas, 102, 103
Schöffer, Nicolas, 102
Schwitters, Kurt, 102, 166
sculpting
    general methods, 61–65, 67, 69–76
    reproduction and surface-finishing techniques, 76, 78–84, 87
sculptural design
    elements of, 1–6
    principles of, 6–8, 10, 12, 14
    relation to other arts, 14, 16
sculptural materials
    primary, 17–27, 31–38
    secondary, 39–42
sculptural use, history of
    in architecture, 25, 34, 120–121

coins, 124
commemorative, 122
decoration, 120
gem and stone carving, 125
in landscaping, 121–122
medals, 124
rituals, 125
sculpture, conservation and restoration, 42–56
sculpture in the round, design principles of, 89–92, 100
Segal, George, 102, 103, 172
Shihuangdi, tomb of, 136
slip casting, 79, 81
Smith, David, 27, 28–30, 76, 113, 168
Smithson, Robert, 104–105, 173
smoothing, 82–83
Spiral Jetty, 105, 173
Stele of Hegeso, 109
stiacciato relief, 99
stone
    conservation and restoration, 43–51
    history of use in sculpture, 17–18, 24
surface finishing, 82
Surrealism, 29, 111, 161, 166, 167, 169
symbolism, 114–116, 118–119

T

terra-cotta, 31, 32–35, 81
Tinguely, Jean, 101
Trajan's Column, 108
Tucker, William, 60
Tula, 127, 128–129
Turnbull, William, 61
tympanum, 115, 117–118

U

United States, sculpture in,
    156–160
Untitled (Plastic Cups), 178

V

Valley Curtain, 105, 175
Venus de Milo, 138
Verrocchio, Andrea del, 10,
    35, 148–149

W

Walking Woman, 163
Wave, 164
wood
    conservation and restora-
      tion of, 54–56
    history of use in sculpture,
      25–26

Z

Zadkine, Ossip, 25